Digital Asset Ecosystems

Chandos
Information Professional Series

Series Editor: Ruth Rikowski
(Email: Rikowskigr@aol.com)

Chandos' new series of books is aimed at the busy information professional. They have been specially commissioned to provide the reader with an authoritative view of current thinking. They are designed to provide easy-to-read and (most importantly) practical coverage of topics that are of interest to librarians and other information professionals. If you would like a full listing of current and forthcoming titles, please visit www.chandospublishing.com.

New authors: we are always pleased to receive ideas for new titles; if you would like to write a book for Chandos, please contact Dr Glyn Jones on g.jones.2@ elsevier.com or telephone +44 (0) 1865 843000.

Digital Asset Ecosystems

Rethinking crowds and clouds

Tobias Blanke

ELSEVIER

AMSTERDAM • BOSTON • CAMBRIDGE • HEIDELBERG • LONDON
NEW YORK • OXFORD • PARIS • SAN DIEGO
SAN FRANCISCO • SINGAPORE • SYDNEY • TOKYO
Chandos Publishing is an imprint of Elsevier

CP
CHANDOS PUBLISHING

Chandos Publishing
Elsevier Limited
The Boulevard
Langford Lane
Kidlington
OX5 1GB
UK
store.elsevier.com/Chandos-Publishing-/IMP_207/

Chandos Publishing is an imprint of Elsevier Limited

Tel: +44 (0) 1865 843000
Fax: +44 (0) 1865 843010
store.elsevier.com

First published in 2014

ISBN: 978-1-84334-716-3 (print)
ISBN: 978-1-78063-382-4 (online)

Chandos Information Professional Series

Library of Congress Control Number: 2014934496

British Library Cataloguing-in-Publication Data.
A catalogue record for this book is available from the British Library.

Typeset in the UK by Concerto.

Contents

List of figures

About the author

Tobias Blanke is a Senior Lecturer in the Centre for e-Research, Department of Digital Humanities at King's College London. He is the director of the MA in Digital Asset and Media Management. His academic background is in philosophy and computer science.

Tobias's principal research interests lie in the development and research of digital libraries and archives, as well as infrastructures for research, particularly in the arts and humanities. Currently, he is working and leading on several projects in the field, from open-source optical character recognition, open linked data and scholarly primitives to document mining and information extraction for research.

Tobias works on several international projects and committees. Most notably, he is one of the directors of the Digital Research Infrastructure for Arts and Humanities (DARIAH), a European initiative to create an integrated research infrastructure for arts, humanities and cultural heritage data. He also leads the joint research work for EHRI, a pan-European consortium to build a European Holocaust Research Infrastructure.

1

Introduction

The idea of digital ecosystems has recently proliferated as a catchphrase in public discussions about concepts such as big data and social media. Big data seems to be everywhere right now. Social media, too, appears as the golden answer of more and more applications and discourses. Both are intrinsically linked and part of the digital ecosystems. As we shall discuss in this book, big data only becomes big if the same action is repeated time and again. It has received so much attention because everyone in the digital public space can experience it on a daily basis in the ever-growing number of tweets, Facebook friends, etc. in social media applications. At the same time, much of the commercial promise of social media and the excitement it generates in outside observers, from sociologists (who want access to free information about people) to marketers (who want to sell products better), is linked to social media generating big data.

According to a *Financial Times* special report (Financial Times, 2012a), big data is empowering individuals, as the analytical techniques that come with it allow them to get a better overview of the distributed knowledge out there, hidden in social media worlds and elsewhere. Businesses are, however, struggling to decode all this data and they are starting to drown in it – 'Businesses are doing their best to store and use that information' (Financial Times, 2012b) – and it seems unclear yet whether they will succeed. What is lacking, according to the FT analysis, is the equivalent of a librarian in a library for the corporate world to exploit all the information they need. 'Masters of big data' (Financial Times, 2012b) will be able to connect with the user and able to navigate the big data space to support this connection. With such masters, users and businesses gain control over the data tsunami they are faced with. This book will discuss how digital ecosystems are created to exploit the economic and societal potential of social media and to master big data.

One example that we shall come back to again and again is Facebook, which has long grown out of its existence as a single web application and become a big data organisation. Recently, the UK's *Guardian* comment section discussed the Facebook Home App, the latest evolution of social media (Poole, 2013). Facebook promises a 'great, living, social phone' so that in those moments when we are not totally occupied with the activities around us, we can escape to its world. But it is not just the real world that Facebook Home protects us from. The online world is also filtered:

> Facebook's use of the word Home for the app does reflect, though, the site's attraction to many of its billion users: that it is the digital world's equivalent of a gated community, or perhaps a padded cell. Facebook is nice because it's comfortingly insulated from the flame wars, gadget reviews, and paedophile rings that make up 99% of the rest of the internet.
>
> (Poole, 2013)

This view of Facebook as a gated community represents the negative idea of what digital ecosystems might be about, as we shall find out in this book. But we can be saved from being enclosed in these gated communities by taking control of our own data as our own curators: 'You too can perfectly well continue to use Facebook... as long as you make sure to curate your data trail with appropriate misdirection' (Poole, 2013). Open ecosystems are the consequence.

Whether we consider ourselves as masters of our own data universe or as enclosed in an online gated community, without doubt we are witnessing a major change in how the World Wide Web is reorganised around us. This will affect all applications on the web, but also what we are mainly interested in here: all the digital content. Both big data and social media are key drivers in this change. This book has been written as we wanted to understand the role of digital assets and digital media in this evolution of the online environment.

If digital assets are, at the most generic level, digital objects with a value that can be economic, social or cultural, plus the correct rights to realise these values, there will be an obvious link to big data and social media. Big data is about extracting all three kinds of value from the large seas of content, while social media is about realising social value online. But digital assets are still connected to social media and big data in another way. They are all parts of the development to separate out the web into larger digital ecosystems; these in turn are the centrepiece of a development to evolve the open digital public space of the World Wide Web into a better value-creating and value-realising entity.

If digital assets are difficult to define, digital ecosystems will be even more so. When researching for this book, it quickly became clear that it would not be productive to advance on an understanding of their impact by giving a fixed definition first. They seem to be such a productive idea, as they are often used with varying meanings in different contexts. In all these meanings, digital ecosystems are considered key to the debate about how best to ensure the productive future of the web – not just in the sense that new business models need to develop, but also in terms of how the web can at the same time keep its original promise to be a neutral platform, available to all.

Digital ecosystems help us understand how the digital value creation and digital asset production evolve on the web because of the synthesis of its two core forces that have helped the web mature. The first one is the development of the web into a digital platform for applications and content. We can use the term 'cloud' for this, as it is more commonly understood. While most encounter the cloud as a dark archive for some of their content, or as a means to shift content between devices, it is much more than that, as we shall see. The second force that has enabled the digital ecosystem revolution is the crowd or the collaboration of large numbers of humans on a common task. Social media as in the Facebook world is one instantiation of the crowd, but there are many others. This includes work for money in what some fear might develop into a global culture of online sweatshops (Horton, 2011), and others hail as the next big thing in the global labour relationships (Scholz, 2012). Common to all these crowd activities is that the task they work on will benefit from many cooks preparing it. Crowds are about collaboration, whatever motivates it.

When investigating the relationship of crowds and clouds in digital ecosystems, it soon became clear that their work is complementary and that they must not be regarded as two separate forces. This book investigates how they are employed together as two sides of the same coin. In this division of work, computers do what they are good at, such as the analysis of large amounts of data, where the data is mined for content, clustered around themes and in general squeezed for anything valuable in it. Crowds do the rest and go where the computers cannot reach at the moment, either because the data is too complex when, for example, handwritten records need to be OCRed, or because deeper meaning needs to be extracted. Crowds also cluster together in groups of friends and colleagues in social media applications, which computers in turn can exploit to recommend them things that these groups like as a whole.

This book will present how crowds and clouds inhabit the digital ecosystem to deliver digital assets into consumption or to understand the consumer of the digital assets better. We see a digital economy developing that is quickly transforming the role of digital assets and making them the centrepiece of the activities within a digital ecosystem. Economists have always known how important the division of labour between humans and machines is for the success in the value production. The same applies to the digital economy; the differences are that here we produce digital assets and the division of labour is one between human crowds and computer machines.

We shall discuss case studies of industries, which can be considered at the forefront of the crowd and cloud division of work, from publishing to media. New publishing models develop right in front of our eyes, and digital media has been for a long time traded on large-scale digital platforms with the active participation of the consumers. In this digital environment, boundaries between producers and consumers of digital assets are often nothing more than temporary arrangements, useful only to understand a digital asset workflow, but not to mark clear and lasting distinctions.

This book aims to reposition digital assets and media in the global workflows and divisions of labour. We are trying to understand the emergence of new digital asset practices and how digital ecosystems and their crowds and clouds are instrumental for the production and consumption of digital assets. To this end, we start our book with a background chapter that at first has to explore what digital assets are. This is far from obvious, and various definitions do not exactly compete with each other, but they can at least be seen as alternatives. We ask what it means to be a digital object with value, and how this value changes when digital assets are taken out of their archives and moved into the global digital networks. Nowadays, it is not enough any more to just think of digital asset management (DAM) as delivering order to an otherwise unorganised heap of digital objects in an organisation. The new emerging, interconnected global workflows of the digital economy need to be considered. This is the reason why we introduced crowds and clouds, as they help us understand these workflows, which for digital asset management in particular mean that we can describe how digital assets and digital media are prepared for production and consumption.

In Chapter 2, we continue to explain why we consider crowds, as a form of global human ubiquitous computing, to be so important to understanding the evolution of digital assets. We also discuss that to us, clouds are much more than what they are commonly known for, such as storage spaces in cyberspace. They need to be understood as the most prominent incarnation of the development of the web into an application platform connected to ubiquitous computing resources, which are heavily interlinked.

There are definitely new technologies and digital methodologies that support digital ecosystems, and without which their idea could not have developed. These technologies include the development of the web from a way to exchange hyperlinked documents to a platform for applications, as well as a way to stay in touch with the things around us in the mobile ecosystem. The mobile ecosystem has become the great mediator of everyday life for hundreds of millions of people and the way they interact with each other and the things around them.

In Chapter 3, we discuss in detail the technologies and methodologies that are enabling the digital ecosystem. We try to understand further the evolution of the web, how web APIs (application programming interfaces) are beginning to change the way we exchange information and applications, and how the web has become something for machines and humans alike. Crowds and clouds come into the mix to add intelligence to content, applications and services. We are only beginning to see the new kinds of technical infrastructures that engage crowds and clouds most effectively.

An absolute must for the engagement of crowds and clouds is that content and, if possible, applications are open, as we analyse in Chapter 4. However, digital ecosystems again add another dimension to these discussions. In order to develop profits based on the web, the future web will entail a combination of open and closed pieces of infrastructure and content. This raises the question as to whether this may undermine its original promises and may therefore lead to its demise. Almost immediately when big web companies introduce a new feature, it is measured against this open web promise, going back to the early days of the web, either by its users or by media observers. Digital ecosystems seem to offer not just a way for companies to relaunch the web into something that can make profit for them while at the same time staying open, but also as a way for us to understand these developments.

Chapter 5 takes us through some of the corresponding debates from open data in sciences and governments to the question of effective use, which is sometimes forgotten. If we consider effective use, we need to include open infrastructures in our debates on open data, which we see as one of the main motivations behind open linked data. Otherwise, filter bubbles and walled gardens develop, and as we shall see, these walls are difficult to tear down.

Open data leads to big data, as all of it is in easy reach. Crowds and clouds contribute to what many consider to be the next big thing, as they support the analysis of big data, and their combination is itself an answer to how big data challenges current computing infrastructures. Once understood from the perspective of crowds and clouds, big data or big content becomes one of the main drivers for the change we are describing. The digital ecosystems we are observing are in many ways set up to deal with big data and make it work as an economic force for change.

Chapter 5 analyses this change by first attempting to define big data from its use. From the history of big data use, we see that it is much older than the current debates might suggest. Science data has been big for a long time and has also driven the innovation of new ecosystems that could make this big data work. Today, many big data challenges are still driven by the demands of extreme science, but also by other big data organisations in business and government. The chapter investigates, together with other business areas, mainly social media applications and some of the current limitations of applying big data analytics here, before concluding with some critical remarks regarding the Big Brother potential behind big data.

Chapter 6 then discusses some of the economic and social concepts linked to digital ecosystems. Next to the already presented division of work, the new phenomenon of free labour is presented, before we come to the kind of value that really seems to matter in the world of crowds and clouds, which is the network value. It describes how the value of digital assets depends more and more on how deeply they are embedded in the global networks and how much they motivate other consumers. The network value plays a role in all applications of digital ecosystems we investigate throughout this book – so much so, that digital assets cannot be discussed any more without considering their network value.

2

Background

Abstract: This book aims to reposition digital assets and media in the global workflows and divisions of labour. We are trying to understand the emergence of new digital asset practices, and how digital ecosystems and their crowds and clouds are instrumental for the production and consumption of digital assets. To this end, we first have to explore what digital assets are. Nowadays, it is not enough to think of digital asset management as just delivering order to an otherwise unorganised heap of digital objects in an organisation. The new emerging, interconnected global workflows of the digital economy need to be considered. Crowds and clouds help us understand these workflows, which means that we can describe how digital assets and digital media are prepared for production and consumption.

We consider crowds as a form of global human ubiquitous computing. As such, they help us understand the evolution of digital assets. To us, clouds are much more than what they are commonly known for, such as storage spaces in cyberspace. They need to be understood as the most prominent incarnation of the development of the web into an application platform connected to ubiquitous computing resources, which are heavily interlinked.

The chapter finally considers two case studies from digital publishing and digital media where crowds and clouds already work together in the new global workflow around digital assets.

Key words: digital ecosystem, crowds, clouds, digital assets, digital media, division of work, pathologies of big data.

The new world of digital assets

This book positions digital assets within the emerging world of digital networks. While digital networks are now part of our everyday experience, digital assets are far less so and have largely escaped attention. On the most general level, they are digital things with value, digitally produced and realised in a digital consumption. If we accept this definition of digital assets, this book will be about how values are realised in networks of consumers and producers of digital objects.

Such consumption can happen in a market setting. This is generally discussed under the concept of monetisation of assets (Austerberry, 2012). Monetisation is an important part of the realisation of digital assets, but we are less interested in it here. Another way of consuming digital assets happens at every transition within the asset life cycle. There are many definitions of this digital life cycle of objects, but they mostly converge on at least creating, managing, discovering and (re) using as essential components of any digital object's life. These are the 'basic stages content moves through from creation to providing ongoing preservation, management and access over time' (LeFurgy, 2012).

Digital asset value stems today not just from direct consumption or monetisation, but also from how digital assets are repurposed in this life cycle in networks. This is a very different way of repurposing their use than traditional sources of digital asset management (DAM) theory would have thought of. Austerberry (2012), one of the main sources for digital asset management theory, offers the following view on the meaning of digital asset value:

> What gives an asset value? If it can be resold, then the value is obvious. However, it can also represent a monetary asset, if it can be cost-effectively repurposed and then incorporated into new material.
>
> (Austerberry, 2012: 5)

This idea needs to be amended, once we take into account that digital asset consumption is not linear and follows a more complex life cycle that is dynamic and evolving in global networks. This chapter will start from the traditional definition of digital assets, but will also present why this definition is not sufficient any more. We investigate how digital assets integrate in digital networks in their life cycle, how they move from place to place and from system to system, and how they pass through the hands of 'dedicated communities' and are, in this way, one of the foundation blocks of something we call the digital asset ecosystem, which we shall define later in this chapter.

In the discipline of digital asset management, a digital asset is often considered to be an enriched digital file. Austerberry (2012) starts his introductory book, *Digital Asset Management*, with a discussion about how digital files become a dominant form of content in an enterprise. 'Content creators and publishers are looking to digital asset management (DAM) to improve productivity and to provide sensible management in a file-based production environment' (Austerberry, 2012: 1). Files are enriched with metadata in order to, for instance, describe an object's identity.

According to this standard definition, digital assets are firstly considered to be files and have a value on their own, as Jacobsen et al. (2005) also state:

> The first definition (asset =file+rights) is more widely used in the context of assets that have a certain value on their own. For example, think of an MP3 file of a song from your favorite band. From a business perspective, it is useless as long as you don't have the right to do something with it...
>
> (Jacobsen et al., 2005: 2)

Jacobsen et al. go on to state that, secondly, digital assets are digital files amended with metadata. They consider this second definition of digital assets to be complementary to the first, as digital assets' metadata is used to describe not only the content of the file, but also the rights attached to it.

Both definitions in these introductory digital asset management books bring together technical elements and conceptual ones. A digital file becomes an asset only because it is enriched with additional information that enables its consumption. It has value and so on. This combination of elements is what interests us, too, but we do not agree with Jacobsen et al. (2005) on the technical dimension of digital assets. Throughout this book, we shall introduce many digital assets that are much more than files, unless one considers everything durable in a computer to be a file. While there is some truth in this, the definition would become too generic. We prefer to speak of digital objects instead of files. Unfortunately, Jacobsen et al. also do not follow up on their second insight that there are conceptual elements in the definition of digital assets. Digital assets are not just files/objects, but only those that are made for consumption by others, that have the correct rights attached to them and the right metadata to find and access them. Metadata has no purpose in itself, but only in the (future) consumption by others, as Gartner et al. (2008) demonstrate.

Jacobsen et al. (2005) produce a workable definition for their purposes, which is to investigate the life of digital assets in a digital asset management (DAM) system. Core components of DAM systems include a repository to manage and store digital assets, a metadata-based catalogue with a search engine for retrieving assets, and finally more advanced features, such as rights management and workflow engines to organise the execution of tasks (Arthur, 2005). With this set-up, DAM systems are designed to manage unstructured information that most likely does not have a predefined data model. This information needs to be enriched in ways that suit the consumption by designated, often rather specific communities. Its most common form is documents of all kinds, either multimedia ones or plain old text ones, where metadata is an essential part of this enrichment. As unstructured information is the predominant form of data in the world, DAM systems in their various forms have therefore become an essential part of the global digital life. Eighty per cent of business information is unstructured (Grimes, 2011), and this percentage only grows with the integration of more and more business cases in the digital world.

Finally, one needs to consider that both introductory DAM books discussed here were published in the mid-2000s. The general use case for digital asset management was then to bring order to the digital files in an organisation, often by using a centralisation strategy (Arthur, 2005). The organisations' general use case in books like *Implementing a Digital Asset Management System* are photo and animation companies that would like to organise their multimedia assets. Digital asset management's return on investment in systemising digital assets is consistency across the organisation, quicker and controlled access to all its files, durable backup, etc. This book will go further and investigate how digital assets appear in the whole network of an organisation's activities on the intranet and Internet, and how they are not just part of a larger product such as picture assets for a digital animation.

DAM systems have evolved from back-office systems to components of the front-office value creation environments (Austerberry, 2012). In many ways, digital assets are actually the objects that keep an organisation together across various digital environments, as we shall discuss in later examples, when we look at data as organisational boundary objects. This is especially true in one of the major industries of the future: digital media. This book is less about the importance of digital assets for individual business endeavours. To us, digital assets are interesting as parts of a larger transformation, at the end of which we shall see a new economy emerging, with digital assets at its heart and based on the close collaboration of humans with computing machines to produce, enrich and consume these digital assets.

The subtitle of our book – rethinking crowds and clouds – indicates the importance we attach to this collaboration for the future of digital asset management and the digital economy as a whole. Mature businesses of the twenty-first century will be successful if they manage to integrate human and computing machines into their production workflows. This is not just the case for the narrower digital economy, but also for other parts of businesses, as software becomes the dominating infrastructure for all businesses (Austerberry, 2012). Digital assets as defined above are excellent cases for this overall development, as they depend on meaningful consumption. For digital assets, we know that machines, for the foreseeable future, will not be able to attach reliable meaning to the complex multimedia objects that dominate the digital asset market. Computers, in particular, struggle with the creativity needed to create valuable digital objects like animation films or to reuse them in new contexts (Levy and Murnane, 2012).

Computers, on the other hand, process with ease the large amounts of information and digital assets that are the result of the global digital environment. We shall discuss the new division of labour, which involves human and computing agents, and will analyse how this division can be productive in digital asset management, but also where the potential dangers and pitfalls are. To us, the idea of digital ecosystems epitomises a new concept of how to accommodate the creative integration of human and computer activities. Research into digital asset management is then also research into processes that integrate computing and human behaviour around digital content. We shall also see throughout this book that this challenge is not unique to digital asset management, but can be found in many areas that will shape the twenty-first century economy and society – areas like big science or e-government.

At the core of this reshaping towards a digital economy and society are the concepts of crowds and clouds, upon which this book is built. Crowds and clouds are used for the management and analysis of vast amounts of data that is insufficiently described as 'big data'. In the next section, we shall analyse current developments in crowd and cloud computing. We consider crowds from an information systems point of view, where they are part of the infrastructure to make the processing and analysis of digital content easier. This is a view best summarised in

Amazon's view of its Amazon Web Services framework in Figure 2.1 (page 14), where the Amazon crowdsourcing service Mechanical Turk is just another application that runs on their cloud infrastructure, on the same level as parallel processing or messaging services. Crowds and clouds need to be thought of together, and Amazon has pioneered this view.

Crowds are the subject of a large sociological literature, often based on work by the French social psychologist, Le Bon. In his 1895 book *The Crowd: A Study of the Popular Mind* (Le Bon, 1897), he famously assumed the crowd to be primitive and intellectually inferior to the individual. Only if it is directed, might anything good come of it. In the late nineteenth and early twentieth century, Le Bon was not alone in his suspicion of the crowd. Nietzsche wanted his Zarathustra to break away from herd mentality (Nietzsche, 2005). Today, crowds are less feared than they were then, although they are still considered to be dangerous when not controlled.

Crowdsourcing offers an opposing view. As we shall see, in their digital forms, crowds are first of all seen as exposing collective intelligence. Furthermore, they are collectively intelligent exactly because they are unorganised and dispersed. New knowledge is therefore hidden in them, and crowds provide answers where other means fail. A crowd's conceptual neighbouring 'communities' could not fill this role, as they commonly describe much more closely knit social entities with a shared understanding. They are crowds with a set purpose. For Le Bon's contemporary, Ferdinand Tönnies (1955), crowds are therefore distinct from societies, where people come together based on their self-interests.

As the history of the modern crowd is fast becoming digital, its advantages compared to communities and isolated individuals have become apparent to its observers. The qualities that once angered Le Bon and Nietzsche are now seen as essential for digital progress.

> Heterogeneous and unstable, [crowds] arise as the result of the promiscuous intermingling... of social classes, age groups, races, nationalities, and genders... They can no longer be perceived as the passive subjects of history... The res publica, or public thing, is now firmly in their hands...
>
> (Schnapp and Tiews, 2006: x)

The 'wisdom of crowds' is celebrated in economic analysis by Surowiecki (2005) and harnessed to enrich digital worlds (Kittur and Kraut, 2008). It is exactly the chaos in the crowd, its dispersedness, its storage of local hidden knowledge, its range of perspectives and maybe even its emotional charge, which digital ecosystems want to plug into. Only like this can crowds be an effective complement of cloud processing, as we shall see.

The Amazon architecture takes the same view and therefore integrates its dispersed local Turk crowds into its cloud services. While crowds and clouds are still more or less separate in the Amazon view, research has already achieved much deeper integration. Franklin et al. (2011) use Amazon's Mechanical Turk to enhance the processing of large-scale databases with crowd knowledge and thus create CrowdDB, because 'some queries cannot be answered by machines only' (Franklin et al., 2011: 61). They implement 'human-oriented query operators to solicit, integrate and cleanse crowd-sourced data' that let the interaction with the crowd seem like any other database work. In this way, they create a data cloud that is able to break out of its own closed world. Databases can only deliver to queries what is stored in them. Crowds happily move to other information sources, should they not find an answer in the first one. The next advantage crowds have is that they can find links between data items that escape the sterility of the formal models that underlie databases. Crowds can make associations and other kinds of 'subjective comparisons'. Challenges to create the CrowdDB include 'answer quality' as well as performance, which depends on crowd worker fatigue or time of the day, as the crowd might be busy elsewhere. The bigger the data and the more unknowns are in the data, the better CrowdDB works.

Crowds and clouds, and how they work together

Crowdsourcing is, in many ways, an old idea. The technique itself goes back to the times of the Babylonians, where a sick person would be left in the street to encounter people who might have had the same symptoms previously and could help with treatment (Stark, 1964). The use of crowds has matured since then (Doan et al., 2011). The modern digital use of the crowd was defined by Jeff Howe in a 2006 article in *Wired* (Howe, 2006). Here, crowds are discussed as an outsourcing strategy. Experts are harnessed for a particular task from the web and their brainpower is used to perform a job otherwise done by paid local employees. Please note that already in this early definition of crowds,

Figure 2.1 AWS infrastructure based on Kalakota (2012)

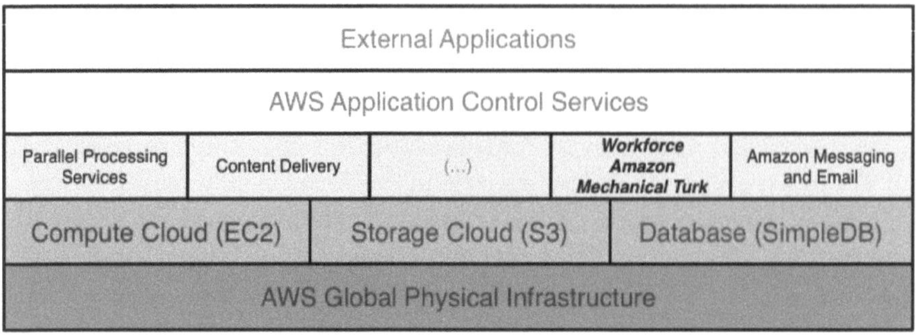

they are needed to address larger tasks and form part of thinking in platforms where computers dominate the workflow and crowds help them with the things that computers cannot do.

The advantages of the digital crowd can be attractive for business. Labour costs can go down significantly. Sometimes one is even able to get 'free labour' from interested parties on the web. 'Free labour' plays an important role in new ideas of generating value from digital assets, as we shall discuss in Chapter 6, where we shall also critique the concept of freedom implied in this kind of labour. Secondly, efforts in businesses can be distributed among those members of a community that might be most effective in executing a particular task and the burden of a large piece of work is shared. We shall come back to these business-oriented questions in Chapter 6. On a less business-oriented level, digital crowds are interesting because everyone can participate. They do not just reduce costs but also harvest ideas. It is this second creative aspect that has started to play an even bigger role in the exploitation of crowds. Collective labour transforms itself into collective intelligence, a concept we shall come back to many times throughout this book.

Malone et al. (2009) have mapped the 'genome of collective intelligence'. They define collective intelligence as 'groups of individuals doing things collectively that seem intelligent' (Malone et al., 2009: 2) and give three convincing reasons why people would like to collaborate to appear intelligent: money; love or enjoyment of an activity; and glory when recognition is achieved among peers. In any case, the crowd is opposed to hierarchical organisation, where a person of authority assigns tasks to the rest. For crowds, anyone can pick up a task. This anti-hierarchy is especially useful if the tasks are not known in advance and the skills needed to perform them are distributed and potentially invisible to the person in authority.

Taking the Amazon infrastructure view, crowds collaborate as part of an emerging larger infrastructure that supports the new kinds of production and consumption of digital value that we can observe. Clouds are part of the same infrastructure and are often even equated with it, although the Amazon view on infrastructure in Figure 2.1 is focused on the difference and limitations of traditional computing infrastructures. Amazon has chosen to offer its crowdsourcing functionalities through the same interface by which its other services are accessible. The substitution of computer intelligence by human intelligence is hidden from the outside world. If the crowds work smoothly, the service seems as automated as a computer service.

While crowdsourcing offers human intelligence resources on demand, cloud computing provides computational resources on demand. Infrastructure has always been most successful if it disappears from view and its use is not noted. As Edwards (2003) has remarked, infrastructures suggest stability in our everyday life:

> [I]nfrastructures are largely responsible for the sense of stability of life in the developed world, the feeling that things work, and will go on working, without the need for thought or action on the part of users beyond paying the monthly bills.
>
> (Edwards, 2003: 188)

Infrastructure makes things work. For instance, the power grid offers this kind of stability; it is simply taken for granted by most, who do not wonder any more why and how it might work. It has become 'unremarkable'. One has got used to the fact that energy is just there. For computing, this has started to become a reality, too. One will not have to worry any more about computing resources, but just plug in to a cloud, which will provide storage or computation on demand. And, if one needs a few more resources, they are also there at the click of a button. This has also been termed 'utility computing' or 'ubiquitous computing', while crowdsourcing has also been called 'ubiquitous human computing' (Zittrain, 2008).

The most comprehensive definition of cloud computing emphasises this view of the stable and universal infrastructure, and comes from the US National Institute of Standards and Technology. The definition concentrates on the utility nature of cloud computing, which is 'a model for enabling ubiquitous, convenient, on-demand network access to a shared pool of configurable computing resources (e.g. networks, servers, storage, applications, and services) that can be rapidly provisioned and released with minimal management effort or service provider interaction' (Mell and Grance, 2011: 2). We shall come back to this definition in Chapter 3, when we discuss cloud computing's technical and methodological framework.

The various types of crowds and clouds are part of the same infrastructure that we have developed to help us with the vast amounts of digitally available content that we produce on a daily basis. This complex has come to be known as 'big data'. We have dedicated all of Chapter 5 to this and only briefly introduce the concept here, in order to understand better what crowds and clouds work on together.

The lexicon of 'big data' has recently proliferated across scholarly and policy arenas. It could have also been called big digital assets or big content, as often multimedia are included next to more traditional types of data, and most of the big data is actually unstructured. For the purposes of this discussion, we shall stick with the generally accepted name and call it 'big data' as well; we shall also discuss, in Chapter 5, the differences between content and data in this context.

Big data is difficult to define, partly because it seems to be an obvious concept. However, as is commonly the case with seemingly obvious concepts that make very good marketing terms, it is far more difficult to analyse. Nevertheless, it seems that nowadays, everybody wants to produce and invest in big data. In the past, it had mainly been a concept discussed and used within quite a narrow technical and scientific community, and it was linked to large-scale science such as the Large Hadron Collider in CERN, the European Organization for Nuclear Research in Geneva. Now, the likes of the *Economist*, Gartner and McKinsey have all come out with a business-oriented special analysis of big data. But big data remains a vague concept. McKinsey's analysts render a widely shared view when they state that big data is 'intentionally subjective and incorporates a moving definition of how big a dataset needs to be' (Manyika et al., 2011: 1). We shall come back to big data's definition in Chapter 5, where we present our own idea of a functional big data definition.

In one of the few more scientific investigations into the concept of big data, Jacobs analyses the *Pathologies of Big Data* (Jacobs, 2009) by running a (thought) experiment on a data set that would cover every single human being. His experiment uses 100 GB 'to store at least the basic demographic information – age, sex, income, ethnicity, language, religion, housing status, and location, packed in a 128-bit record – for every living human being on the planet'. In the end, we have 'a table of 6.75 billion rows and maybe 10 columns'. This would still not really be big data if one simply considers the required storage space; also processing of these kinds of data could be done using quite standard computing equipment. There is no need for complicated ecosystems. Jacobs concludes:

> By such measures, I would hesitate to call this big data, particularly in a world where a single research site, the LHC (Large Hadron Collider) at CERN (European Organization for Nuclear Research), is expected to produce 150,000 times as much raw data each year.
> (Jacobs, 2009: 38)

What Jacobs is stressing is that technology and conventional ideas of size are not the answer if we try to define what big data is.

Rather, we need to think big data in terms of what computers can store and process, and what humans can analyse in their current state of the art, or from the point of view of crowds and clouds. The ability to consume big data is directly linked to the ability to mix human and machine ubiquitous computing and therefore reinvent the infrastructure itself. According to Jacobs, '[b]ig data should be defined at any point in time as data whose size forces us to look beyond the tried-and true methods that are prevalent at that time' (Jacobs, 2009: 44). Data is therefore big not just in terms of the amount we have, but also in terms of what we would like to do with it, how we would like to extract value from it and how we can afford infrastructures that support this extraction of value. Size is relative to the infrastructures we can make from crowds and clouds that allow us to generate new opportunities from big data.

In this sense, the idea of big data challenges digital asset management, not just in terms of digital content size, but mainly because new ways of producing and exploiting data and content need to be invented, as we shall discuss in Chapter 5. This has a direct impact on the central question of digital asset management: the value of digital content. Big data adds new types of value. Opportunities for creating value from big data are manifold, as we present in detail in Chapter 5. Commonly cited examples include the UK retailer Tesco. Its analysis of customer behaviour has helped it increase its sales and improved its marketing strategies (Rowley, 2005). More generally, social network sites such as Facebook and Twitter are analysed by hundreds of often small to medium-sized companies around the world, to monitor consumer behaviour or spot new trends. Jansen et al. (2009) have analysed microblogging online tools for word-of-mouth communication on brands and their perceptions. They have shown how microblogging has quickly become an essential component of marketing strategies.

Boardrooms generally get excited because big data works where future growth promises to be. According to McKinsey's analysis (Manyika et al., 2011), the big data potential value index is particularly high in those areas of the economy such as health care, finance or information processing and management, which have contributed most to the growth of productivity in the USA. All of these face a tsunami of content that, once mastered, will allow new types of value to present themselves. Then there are the concerns that many see in big data – mainly the dreams of Big Brother come true. This goes so far that companies like Google do not want to be publicly associated with big data, as we shall see in Chapter 5.

In order to develop these opportunities from big data, McKinsey (Manyika et al., 2011) recommends developing data-driven organisations and enterprises. As a first step, a digital asset and data audit is implemented to make use of big data. The next step towards the data-driven enterprise is to create new data assets in such a way that they can be reused in networks and that new value can be produced. The digital asset manager needs to be involved in the overall data strategy to master big data, as all these elements need to be linked together. Big data or big assets are only as useful as their consumption.

Digital asset management needs to include an analysis of big data, not least because its main concern are multimedia files, and these are what have contributed most to the recent spikes in data production. Often cited is the fact that 48 hours of video are uploaded to YouTube every minute (Wittaker, 2012). It might be, however, less known that video also dominates already data-rich sectors such as health care. In surgeries, high-resolution videos result in 25 times more data volume (per minute) than CT scans, which produce still images (Manyika et al., 2011: 21); more than 95 per cent of clinical data is now video-based. The data stored by companies around the world exceeded 6 exabytes in 2010 (Manyika et al., 2011: 15), equivalent to filling 60,000 US Libraries of Congress.

These kinds of big data stories have been brewing for a while and have reached all parts of economy and society now. A few years ago, Hal Varian from Google and Peter Lyman from the University of California, Berkeley conducted research into the question of just how much big data is out there. As part of their 'How much information?' project, they estimated that 5 exabytes of new data had already been created in 2002 and that new data was being developed at a growth rate of 25 per cent (Lyman and Varian, 2003). In this sense, big data is already old.

Digital asset management theory and practice is closely linked to opportunities that arise from big data, according to McKinsey's analysis (Manyika et al., 2011). It helps us to understand what the impact of big data on digital asset management for the business community might be. We can use some of McKinsey's points on big data and easily map them to the digital asset and media management world:

- Big data will better support transparency of digital content by integrating different data sets and providing easier access to them. The time required to search and find the right information is reduced immensely. In the field of digital asset management, this would mean that one has easier access to the right digital assets one needs for the production of an animation film or a marketing campaign. Furthermore, one has a greater choice of digital assets available and can potentially save on licences and avoid the risk of using digital assets with unclear rights attached to them. These are all items that could have come straight from a digital asset management textbook.
- Big data will help segment populations to customise actions, which means that one can target specific groups. For digital asset management, this implies that marketing assets can be better targeted or that digital assets can be more effectively distributed to relevant consumption groups. For instance, Netflix is a video-on-demand (VOD) company that employs complicated algorithms to suggest relevant films to customers, based on their past behaviour. This clustering of digital assets for specific consumer groups is nowadays commonplace and has proven to increase consumption significantly. We shall come back to this in Chapter 4.
- Big data will enable clustering of digital assets for specific consumer needs, which is directly linked to a third area the McKinsey report mentions. Big data creates value, if computers can use these large data sets to support decisions about critical business functions using complex statistical algorithms. The more input data these computers have, the better they will work. For digital asset management, processes that are heavily dependent on human labour can be better supported. For instance, although assigning metadata remains a task for a human in the foreseeable future, today there is already a plethora of tools that support this task by analysing large data sets. Chapter 4 will explore this issue further.

- Big data will support the innovation of new business models, products and services. Our contention is that once we analyse digital assets in the context of the larger digital economy and the digital ecosystems that drive them, completely new services and ideas emerge. The McKinsey report quotes location-aware services as an example. These are by now expected components of the promotion of digital assets, if, for instance, art is advertised on the web together with the next exhibition where a potential customer can buy it. This book addresses many new services based on the new big data, from social curation in social media ecosystems to collective intelligence services for producers of animation films.

Digital asset and media management has a key role to play not only in the development of opportunities from big data, but also in several of the challenges that emerge from it. We shall analyse in Chapter 5 that while some big data challenges are new, many are inherited from the old data world, too. Among these inherited challenges are, as already mentioned, new regulations around data, which need to balance the new demand for data with the essential concerns many people have in terms of security, privacy, etc. Data policy is not just a question of ensuring privacy; in the age of digital reproducibility of creative and artistic work, more fundamental questions may need to be answered. How can the current level of creative work be maintained and even expanded as long as the value extracted from them is mainly attached to the process of distributing them? Artistic and creative work is currently paid for through contracts with its distributors, which are agencies, publishers, etc. The Internet has lowered the costs of distribution so much that it seems that this revenue stream is drying out. However, this might well be too quick a conclusion. Distribution over the Internet requires careful strategies and the involvement of new technology platforms and communities, as we shall discuss in Chapter 3, and these in turn need novel types of mediators. It seems to be much more a changing rather than disappearing landscape, for distributing mediators of digital content. Data and content policies are at the heart of this, but sometimes one needs to wonder whether the relevant distribution industries have realised that these data policies need to work within the new ecosystem and not try to prevent it.

With the advent of technologies like cloud computing, access to data is less of a technical problem than ever. Yet, it has become an even more pressing social problem that requires complex structures of trust and security, at the centre of which is the question of whether to share the data or not. A repository project for science data once gained fame in the context of open data stores with a call to arms for open data: 'The coolest thing to do with your data will be thought of by someone else' (Wikipedia, 2013b). In the world of science this is probably true, though even here the incentives to share one's data are lower than one might assume. Michael Ashburner of the University of Cambridge famously stated that 'biologists would rather share their toothbrush than share a gene name' (Pearson, 2001). In the commercial world, however, the business model that clearly demonstrates the benefits of opening access to data is still to be invented. There are good reasons to share efforts in research and development, for instance, but these fields remain isolated. We shall see later in this book how digital ecosystems have gained new significance in the attempt to build walled gardens around the companies' valuable big content. In order to discuss this, however, we need to investigate first what digital ecosystems entail.

Digital ecosystems

Big data challenges traditional computing infrastructure and requires close collaboration between crowds and clouds. Only if both manage to work together can the opportunities from big data develop. A new division of labour between humans and computers is emerging that is best expressed in the idea of and the research on digital ecosystems. In their 2011 book *Race Against the Machine: How the Digital Revolution is Accelerating Innovation, Driving Productivity, and Irreversibly Transforming Employment and the Economy*, the MIT economists Brynjolfsson and McAffee ask how human labour can survive when faced with the pressures from the computerisation of work. Their answer is that any degree of computerisation still requires human creativity and entrepreneurs in the process of collaboration. 'There has never been a better time to be a talented entrepreneur' (Brynjolfsson and McAfee, 2011: 56). One might disagree with the authors as to whether the current times of austerity are good times for innovation, but creativity seems to remain a human domain. The understanding of computational creativity is still in its infancy (Jordanous, 2010).

Only if we manage to integrate human innovation with computing power will we be able to create successful digital economies of the future. 'New platforms leverage technologies to create marketplaces... by bringing together machines and human skills in new and unexpected ways' (Brynjolfsson and McAfee, 2011: 56). This is true for any activity in the digital economy, but especially true for an economy of digital assets, which will only work if we bring together the abilities of humans to create meaning in new and unexpected ways with the ability of computers to distribute this meaning and maintain it on a large scale. The definitions of digital assets discussed above have indicated that. Brynjolfsson and McAfee consequently cite the 'creation of digital ecosystems' (Brynjolfsson and McAfee, 2011: 56) as a way forward for a new collaboration between humans and computers. To us, this term describes perfectly the answers we can give to opportunities and challenges of big data.

In order to understand these answers, we first need to decode the concept of digital ecosystems, as it is yet another highly overloaded term in computing research.

> The concept digital ecosystem has no single definition, because it seems self-explanatory and because [it] is everywhere, and through widening usage, threatens to become everything, growing popular reference to the digital ecosystem without general agreement on its scope threatens to render the concept increasingly more vague and drained of meaning.
>
> (Zhang and Jacob, 2011)

However, vagueness is not necessarily a problem, as some of the most productive terms in the computing world are based on rather vague definitions. We have just discussed this for big data and there are many more we will meet in this book, such as ontologies or Web 2.0. So, let us not be too discouraged here.

One dominant form of defining digital ecosystems uses the term to describe research into artificial life forms in order to find inspiration from the biological ecosystem for improving computing processes (Briscoe and Sadedin, 2009). This is not the field we would like to focus on. It would lead us away from digital assets and deep into the world of artificial intelligence. In a much looser sense and less connected to biological ecosystems, digital ecosystems describe the connections between networks of platforms, software and users. The idea of a biological ecosystem is still the inspiration though, as these connections between networks are also described by the typical attributes of biological ecosystems like interdependence, heterogeneity, emergence or self-organisation. According to Briscoe and Sadedin (2009), a natural environment consists of ecosystems, which in turn are inhabited by habitats and communities (see Figure 2.2). It is easy to form an analogy here so that populations are our crowds, while the habitats are the platforms/clouds our crowds work on. Together, communities and habitats build niches or, in our sense, applications and services.

Early definitions of digital ecosystems as in E. Chang and West (2006) take this metaphor of the biological ecosystem for the digital world further. They give four 'essences' of both a digital and a biological ecosystem.

1. It is balanced.
2. It is self-organised.
3. It is clustered in domains that are loosely coupled.
4. Its members are engaged in permanent interaction.

This makes the whole of the ecosystem stable against problems of its parts. The biological derivation of digital ecosystems, however, only takes us that far. As with many concepts in computing, the uses of the concept allow us to better understand its meaning. Beyond its theoretical development, the idea of digital ecosystems is best expressed in its dominant current practices.

The practice of digital ecosystems has gained strong momentum in social media. In a 2011 BBC documentary, *Inside Facebook* (BBC, 2012), Mark Zuckerberg described how Facebook's development is dependent on a community of developers outside the company. He compared the number of engineers working for Facebook with those working for Google and Microsoft, and concluded that only a relatively small number of engineers work for Facebook compared to the other big names in the IT industry. His main point is that Facebook relies on a network of developers around their products to improve them continuously.

Figure 2.2 allows us to explain Zuckerberg's idea. Facebook is an environment that helps develop ecosystems for developer and user crowds to inhabit. This takes place in the habitats or platforms the Facebook ecosystem provides, for which we can also use the more popular term 'cloud'. The aim is to find a niche in the Facebook ecosystem and to fill it with one's own ideas, applications and services. In the practices of social media, digital ecosystems have become this gathering of crowds of users and developers around (cloud) platforms such as Facebook's. In *Inside Facebook*, Zuckerberg promised that Facebook was a social experience not just for its millions of users, but also for engineers, who could collaborate to develop applications around it. So, with Facebook

Figure 2.2 From biological to digital ecosystems based on Briscoe et al. (2011)

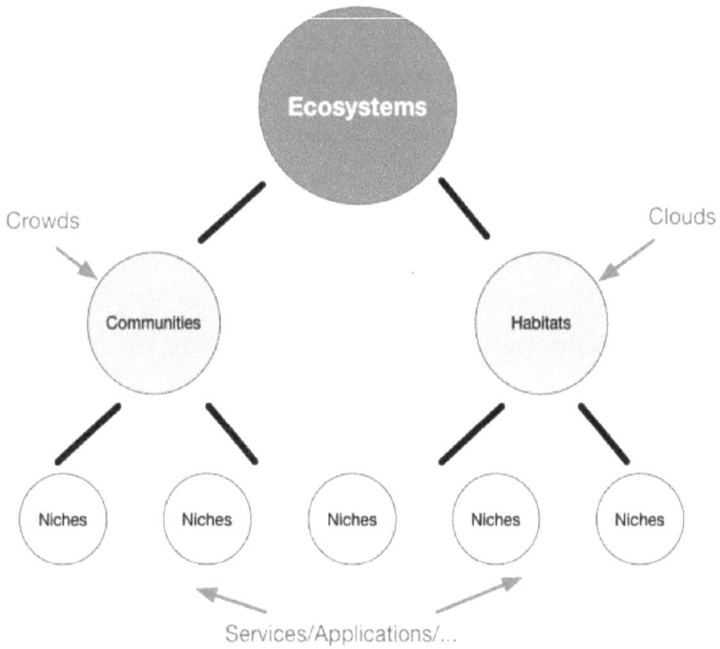

floated on the stock market, people buy stocks that take a bet on the future of large-scale social engineering and socio-technical developments that are common to all digital ecosystem practices.

The Institute of Electrical and Electronics Engineers (IEEE), one of the powerhouses of computing knowledge, agrees with Zuckerberg's idea on digital ecosystems. According to its IEEE Digital Ecosystem conference, digital ecosystems are 'loosely coupled, domain-specific [...] communities which offer cost-effective digital services and value-creating activities' (IEEE Digital Ecosystem, 2007). The interesting idea behind this definition is to derive digital ecosystems from communities, or crowds with a set purpose, rather than technologies, just like in the Facebook case, where Mark Zuckerberg first associates developers and users with digital ecosystems, because in the digital ecosystem they define their services and take control. Therefore, the technologies of the digital ecosystem need to be thought of from the perspective of the crowds and do not define what crowds are.

The second part of this IEEE definition specifies the idea of digital ecosystems as made up of value-creating activities and takes us therefore close to digital asset management theory and practice. In the context of this particular idea of digital ecosystems, the concept of them has been specified to business ecosystems, which is one of the many meanings that the term 'ecosystem' has taken in practice. It helps describe dynamic business interactions between crowds. According to Dini and Nicolai, 'the concept of the business ecosystem... uses ecosystem as a metaphor to capture the dynamic interactions between socio-economic agents and actors' (Dini and Nicolai, 2007: 4). The concept of the ecosystem therefore seems to be successful at describing not just technical but also social dynamisms.

The World Economic Forum (WEF) attaches great value to the further development of business digital ecosystems. It wants us to understand the digital ecosystem in terms of interaction between user and producer crowds, as well as the computing platforms these interactions take place on and the (business) values these produce. A report by the World Economic Forum (2007) discusses the short-term future of the political battle over online services that underlie the concept of digital ecosystems. The WEF ask the following questions:

- Will the digital ecosystems evolve towards more open or closed systems?
- Will the digital business environment become closed or defined by open standards and services?
- Will digital ecosystems come from organic communities or will they be the result of the monopolisation of the digital space by a few large corporations?
- Will only established players or new communities collaborate in the digital ecosystems space?

The WEF is inclined towards the open ecosystem, as this will ensure that digital value-production is extended towards small and medium-sized enterprises, and not enclosed within a small circle of the usual suspects.

In the business digital ecosystem, co-production should be the norm for creating business value (Scheithauer et al., 2011), as crowds dominate. Value is co-produced between the different parts of the crowds, as just discussed for *Inside Facebook*. Co-production also appears to lead to greater value for a longer period of time (Dini et al., 2011: 2): 'Greater collaboration within a particular geographical region or virtual community leads to sustainability of economic growth and enhances the competitiveness of that region or online community.' Therefore, the promise of a new kind of value in the digital ecosystem is not just a question for big business. As Dini et al. have shown, it is especially the small and medium enterprises that can benefit from these developments and compete in a globalised economy (Dini et al., 2011). We therefore should not limit ourselves to examples from big corporations when investigating how value is produced in digital ecosystems. We can extend our investigation to completely new business domains and find out how co-production of value happens here between crowds and clouds.

As with many technological and economic evolutions, the research sector is currently taking a lead in developing productive digital ecosystems in many small experimental projects that lead to new research values. The vision of a digital asset ecosystem is already taking shape in various research domains, especially in developments towards virtual health care. For instance, the UK, Sweden and other European countries have made the virtual integration of digital health assets a priority. There are many examples on a local and international level, and digital ecosystems play an important role bringing together resources for regions of the EU. Serbanati et al. (2011) report, for instance, on a digital health ecosystem for an Italian region structured around the digital health assets. This project exhibits on a small scale all the elements we have discussed for digital ecosystems, such as the use of advanced network technologies and crowdsourcing. In particular, the work with patients is organised around virtual health care records, which display a patient's history of treatment as well as their movements through various health care institutions in the region.

For the purposes of this book, we are less interested in the research applications and more in changes in economic and information activities. Here, there are currently two big drivers behind the integration of digital assets in ecosystems: digital publishing and media. For digital publishing, DAM (digital asset management) systems take centre stage as platforms for pushing rich multimedia contents to a range of consumption devices. In digital media, we can see a more distributed platform based on software services that is worked on by an equally distributed crowd.

The practice of digital ecosystems in media and publishing

The publishing ecosystem has now become digital. This does not mean that all the activities within publishing have become digital or that e-books as its most visible signs will replace printed books completely any time soon. This would be pure speculation. Rather, most of the processes within publishing are now digital and are linked to each other in large-scale computational platforms. Software is the major infrastructure for publishing, and software services bind these software elements together.

In debates about digital publishing, there is a lot of focus on e-book readers and the question whether the publishing industry will soon struggle to maintain its income when faced with the pressures from freely available content from the web. At times, these debates proceed as if e-book readers had fallen from the sky and were not the logical continuation of efficiency drives in publishing, which meant that everything in publishing is organised and run digitally. That is one reason why many publishing houses now use digital asset management systems for all their production processes (Gill, 2005). In fact, e-book readers are the logical consumption end point from digital publishing workflows and advancement into the final bastions of the analogue world, which are based on the way humans best consume information.

There is more to the change of digital publishing ecosystem than e-books. Lichtenberg (2010) explains that the current dynamics of the 'changing ecology of digital publishing' mean that all parties in the digital publishing ecosystem will need to adjust and find new ways forward. But he does not believe that the digital will provide some kind of magic cure for current problems with the publishing business model.

> To be sure, the arrival of the iPad this spring, and the near total absorption on the part of the large trade houses on the pricing issues of the agency model – publishers set the price (within limits) and Apple takes its 30% cut of the sale – has made digital seem like a tsunami poised to wreak havoc on those unfortunates not able to get to higher ground.
>
> (Lichtenberg, 2010: 112)

Nonetheless, it seems unlikely that the printed book will completely disappear any time soon. Instead, new mixed models of publishing have already appeared.

So far, consumers seem happy to pay for interactive, mixed media content, and they seem to like the idea of mixed bundles of print and digital content (Kon et al., 2010). In their study for the Wyman Group on the digital future of publishing, Kon et al. (2010) came to the conclusion that publishing models, which have simply mapped the existing analogue way of publishing onto the digital world by putting the same content online using formats such as PDF, have not only failed to convince consumer crowds, but have also contributed massively to the decline in publishing revenues, not least because the added value of these kinds of online activities can be copied easily. Consumers have, however, been happy to pay for enhanced content that allows for the integration of multimedia and interactive content.

The growing pressure to link traditional document formats with multimedia content is one reason for the rise of digital asset management solutions for publishing. They have become essential publishing platforms. DAM systems hide the differences between traditional document formats and new multimedia content, and allow for an integration of content across the publishing ecosystem (Carreiro, 2010). This shift for DAM systems to become centre stage is particularly obvious in magazine publishing, where the latest innovations have led to rich interactive experiences integrating video content with flexible navigation features and high levels of personalisation. The weekly *Newsweek* is now published only on the iPad and does not appear in a printed version any more (Preston, 2012). Magazine publishing in the digital ecosystem is, however, not an easy marriage, as the recent demise of the iPad-only newspaper *The Daily* has shown (Sweney, 2012). A general lack of original digital content was blamed by media analysts for the end of *The Daily*. However, future promises seem to outweigh these initial setbacks.

According to the already cited study by the Wyman Group, using a simulation on subscriptions for magazines (Kon et al., 2010), interactive periodicals are the first traditional publishing medium to benefit fully from the high-quality enhanced content. The study has reached a series of interesting findings, showing the following:

- Renewal rates to magazine subscriptions can be increased by using interactive content by up to 70 per cent in particular groups.
- Providing rich interactive content can justify a price premium, as some consumers are happy to pay extra to have access to additional digital content next to their standard subscription.
- Cross-selling is made easier by using information from the digital behaviour of consumers (for instance, which articles they look at for how long) in order to enable the recommendation of subscriptions to other related magazines.

Using rich interactive content also means that digital content is not seen as an alternative to print any more. Many customers choose to keep their print subscriptions because of the rich interactive additional content (Kon et al., 2010).

Digital asset management is very important for these kinds of new opportunities of integrating content in the publishing ecosystem, as it enables support of all the key ingredients of growth opportunities in rich interactive publishing. It helps with the development of new products from existing assets, and makes it easy to republish content assets in different interactive contexts, offering many sampling opportunities. The Wyman Group study concludes that 'many [publishing] ecosystem participants are looking to capitalise on this opportunity and are investing aggressively to enable new interactive reading experiences that reflect and embrace the nature of periodical publishing' (Kon et al., 2010). Similar arguments apply to the second example of digital ecosystems we discuss here: the media ecosystem.

The media ecosystem is another field where recent advancements in technology platforms have led to a large increase in participation by crowds that were previously uninvolved. In the digital publishing world, this has meant the vertical integration of businesses using digital asset management systems to bridge the divide between new and old types of content. In media, the new ecosystem has led to the blurring of traditional boundaries between media production and consumption. To tear down these boundaries, (digital) media applications have begun to make use of new service-oriented technologies. These will be discussed in Chapter 3 in more detail. For now, it suffices to know that with new digital services, every single piece of software and data becomes reusable in new contexts, while services are exposed to each other through common interfaces. Services allow for highly distributed software components that are independent. Thus, traditional consumers of media content can become producers, because their contributions can be captured independently from other core production services. All this becomes possible because traditional hierarchies between those who serve and those who are served disappear in the digital ecosystem, as already envisioned in the idea of collective intelligence.

This adherence to a common interface is the main concession that an underlying functionality needs to make, to be integrated in the service world. Together, these distributed services are the platform on which the digital media crowds operate, and consumers and producers can contribute on an equal footing. They are true collaborating crowds beyond hierarchies, as noted by Malone et al. (2009). Any application can then combine consumer and producer services freely as distinct units that are data or functionality services and that can be distributed flexibly on a network. The architect of these applications becomes a composer of these services, with the final aim that the services can compose themselves and link their own data and functionality to related services. This kind of composition of applications by (re)using services has been well established for some time in online news services, travel applications or complex everyday finding-out-about applications, such as locating the nearest restaurant or determining the value of local properties.

Commenting on the elimination of traditional boundaries between media producers and consumers through services, John Naughton has aptly described the new relationship between consumers and producers in the media world:

> It's a truism that our communications environment is changing. It was ever thus: all old media were new media once. But there is something special about our present situation at the beginning of the 21st century. The combination of digital convergence, personal computing and global networking seems to have ratcheted up the pace of development and is giving rise to radical shifts in the environment.
>
> (Naughton, 2006: 1)

Naughton believes that the changes we are seeing in media are best studied using the ecosystem framework, as an ecosystem is never static and exhibits many dynamic relationships between communities and their habitats. New software services enable a media information environment that is changing from being dominated by a 'push' of information to customers in a traditional broadcasting world to a 'pull' environment, where customers choose to pick up pieces of information on the web. This also changes the complexities of marketing and advertising, as we shall see in many examples throughout this book.

With this change from a push- to a pull-model of communication in the media ecosystem comes a change in the politics of 'gatekeepers of information', as Naughton calls them. The same crowds that create the information have also become the editors and curators of this information and media assets, for which Naughton cites the blogosphere as an example. In this way, media wealth is created in networks, and the ecosystem of publishing becomes more diverse and richer:

> The new ecosystem will be richer, more diverse and immeasurably more complex because of the number of content producers, the density of the interactions between them and their products, the speed with which actors in this space can communicate with one another, and the pace of development made possible by ubiquitous networking. The problem – or challenge, to use the politically-correct term – is whether business models can be adapted to work in the new environment.
>
> (Naughton, 2006)

By increasing the density of interactions between content producers, wealth is created in the media ecosystem. We shall look at this again in Chapter 6, where we shall analyse the implications of an ecosystem economy of digital assets where everyone owns the productive means to create their own assets.

The creation of wealth in media ecosystems is also emphasised in the research of Hanna et al. (2011), which showcases various examples of media ecosystems in social media advertising. In terms of the new media ecosystem, the media industry needs to learn how to deal with the end of control of their own digital assets, and the end of the rule of experts that guide the opinion of the consumers of these digital assets. It is another sign of the digital ecosystem that the dividing line between the expert and the amateur, not just between producers and consumers of media, is breaking apart. Deuze (2008) calls this 'liquid journalism' for the media world, where 'knowledge about any given topic or subject is based on the ongoing exchange of views, opinions and information between many' (Deuze, 2008: 858). DAM-based publishing of digital content will be key to new 'rich forms of transmedia storytelling including elements of user control and "prosumer"-type agency'. Today, everyone can be a curator of information and media.

Clark and Aufderheide (2009) offer in their report an overview of the new ways in which social media-based ecosystems can develop 'publics around problems', and argue that 'multiplatform, participatory, and digital, public media 2.0 will be an essential feature of truly democratic public life from here on in. And it'll be media both for and by the public' (Clark and Aufderheide, 2009: 2). The media consumer is no longer a passive element, but is in the middle of a cycle of media curation and creation. Media is not simply broadcast to consumers; they actively choose the content that interests them, via either news search sites or their social connections. Another sign for the participatory character of the new media ecosystem is therefore the continuous discussions taking place on various media sites that are distributed across different types of media. Nowadays, this means the combination of various channels, where tweets are reused in blogs, while blogs have long become part of the everyday online representation of newspapers and magazines.

News is therefore 'collaboratively created', not just on the big topics, but at a local level, too. The collaborative work is often assessed by peers in the media ecosystem, and ranked and reviewed through various technical means. Users often trust other users more and have taken over the curation of the content themselves. They have taken away the power from traditional mediators such as travel book companies or official hotel classification. According to Clark and Aufderheide (2009), all this is done on top of new platform technologies that allow for the collaborative storage and distribution of large-scale media objects, the clouds and other data systems, which we shall discuss in more detail in the next chapter.

Only with the development of these cloud platforms and data back-ends has it become possible to exchange large multimedia files such as videos easily and to enrich the media ecosystem with visual grass-roots reporting. For the emergence of the 'ubiquitous video', it is key that technology platforms can guarantee near twenty-four-hour service. For YouTube and Facebook, it is often less important what the latest tool might offer users compared to the requirement that the services should never be down, to allow for a continuous formation of publics. Only with the clouds could data-intensive visual reporting also become commonplace for niche crowds and fulfil Latour's prediction on the importance of objects and things for public space. YouTube and Facebook then produce the 'objects... [that] bind all of us in ways that map out a public space' (Latour, 2005: 5).

Clark and Aufderheide (2009) quote two more essential requirements for an open social media ecosystem, which we shall meet more often throughout the rest of this book. Firstly, the systems and content need to be open, as otherwise they cannot be customised by the niche crowds to fulfil their application requirements, and secondly, the digital media content needs to move completely into the cloud, because only then can it be shared easily between users and devices.

This vision of the new evolving media ecosystem (Gillmor, 2008) implies the participatory creation of stories and 'networked communities that value conversation, collaboration and egalitarianism over profitability' (Bowman and Willis, 2003: 12). Thus, for some, this hails 'the kind of media that political philosophers have longed for' (Clark and Aufderheide, 2009: 11). This is at least the optimistic view that business white papers like to take. However, this is only one side of the story. As we shall discuss later on, a much more critical stand on contributions by free labour is needed. In the optimistic spirit of some contributors, Bowman and Willis (2003) believe that the digital media ecosystem compares to free conversations in public market places, while John Naughton (2006) sees Habermas' idea of a public space best realised in the new media ecosystem.

According to Habermas, when individuals meet to form a public body, a public sphere is realised. But a public sphere can only develop when citizens can 'confer in an unrestricted fashion' (Habermas et al., 1974: 49). Habermas goes on to cite traditional media as public spheres and excludes state authority from it, as the public sphere is meant to control its authority and institutionalise supervision. At the same time, Habermas also warns that large corporations and other interest groups have taken over the public sphere and re-feudalised it to one where private interests dominate, rather than the free exchange of citizens. This is because the large media has been taken over by private interest. In this sense, one can really assume that the new Web 2.0 worlds might provide a counterweight, since access to the public sphere is, to an extent, democratised. Publishing media has become more accessible than ever before, and grass-roots reporting can take place.

Journalists have always transmitted media objects. But their pathways have never encountered such a large group of protagonists and antagonists. This includes production and consumption. Grass-roots reporting has matured, and bloggers and blog indices are now important parts of the news and digital media production cycle. Designated online communities will comment, analyse and check facts coming out of professional media productions. We have only begun to understand the importance of this development.

This chapter has begun with trying to understand some of the uncertainties that are linked to the ideas of digital assets and digital ecosystems. Both ecosystems and digital assets escape conventional attempts to define them, particularly since digital assets have become parts of digital ecosystems. A digital asset is then still a digital object with value, but this relation has become much more complicated, because the life cycle of digital assets extends beyond the boundaries of organisations and is embedded in digital ecosystems. Crowds and clouds are driving this change, and are at the same time driven by it. Here, it is especially the integration of human intelligence in the global computing networks that has opened the door for new applications to emerge in the context of the big data challenge. Big data is not just about size, but also about new computing infrastructures. Digital ecosystems are templates of how crowds and clouds can work together to address big data. We finally discussed Facebook's interpretation of digital ecosystems, as well as two practical examples of existing digital ecosystems in publishing and media.

3

Methodologies and technologies

Abstract: In this chapter, we discuss in detail the technologies and methodologies that are enabling the digital ecosystem. We try to understand further the evolution of the web, how web APIs (application programming interfaces) are beginning to change the way we exchange information and applications, and how the web has become something for machines and humans alike. Crowds and clouds come into the mix to add intelligence to content, applications and services. We are only beginning to see the new kinds of technical infrastructures that engage crowds and clouds most effectively.

Key words: web evolution, web standards, web architecture, cloud computing, crowdsourcing, programmable web, APIs.

A web for machines and humans alike

This chapter is not intended to offer a general introduction into web technologies, digital services and all the other digital ecosystem technologies. These introductions can be found in numerous forms and shapes elsewhere. Rather, this chapter focuses on the concepts necessary to understand how the digital asset and media ecosystem can evolve, as we have just discussed for publishing and media, and how it is based on established technologies and methodologies. We shall concentrate on what can be called the best possible web for humans by making the interaction with the web truly interactive, using rich Internet technologies and methodologies. Perhaps even more important is that the web has lost its focus on the human as the main end point of its communication flow and has added machines, which could consume the web's information. The web has become programmable, as we shall discuss.

In 2008, various technical sources started discussing a web-oriented architecture (McKendrick, 2008). Together with the better-known service-oriented architecture (Webber et al., 2010), this web-oriented one contains many of the components of the World Wide Web, which we take for granted today and which has enabled many of the revolutions we have witnessed over the past years. At the centre of this architecture lies the dissemination of intelligence and new protocols to dispersed resources across the web. However, the architecture also mentions new waves of intelligence and digital content accessible via open APIs (application programming interfaces), distributed via the by now omnipresent apps and brought together in user-centric mashups. All of these have made it possible to add intelligence and distributed resources to the web, using human and machine thinking. In this chapter, we shall first discuss a few of the World Wide Web basics before entering the world of the programmable web. This background is important as a starting point for developing a conceptual framework in order to understand digital ecosystems.

Since its beginnings, the web has followed the client and server model. A client communicates with a smart server using the HyperText Transfer Protocol (HTTP) (Webber et al., 2010). They exchange documents marked up in the HyperText Markup Language (HTML). These documents have links with each other and are therefore 'hypertexts'. This architecture of the World Wide Web has proven to be extremely powerful, and has taken years to mature and be accepted. HTTP is today so dominant that most do not even remember the many alternatives that have existed for many years. There are the better-known ones like FTP (file transfer protocol), and the less well-known like SFTP (simple file transfer protocol), or NNTP (network news transfer protocol), as well as many others.

Essentially, the whole web is designed to exchange hypertext documents and has not evolved into another substantial form since its early incarnation as a means to distribute academic document outputs. A client, using a browser, could download these documents from a server. Over time, the server has become smarter and could serve dynamic documents, depending on user requests. It has finally proven to be most efficient in keeping the underlying data in safe data stores (such as databases) and creating the corresponding web pages on the fly.

This development has led to the currently dominating LAMP architecture for web applications, which is an abbreviation based on the first four letters of the most common open-source technologies in the World Wide Web (Ramana and Prabhakar, 2005):

- Linux, the operating system most web servers run on.
- Apache web server technology, used in more than half of all web applications.
- MySQL, the dominating open-source database technology recently acquired by Oracle.
- PHP, Perl or Python, the three main web programming languages.

All these technologies imply easy availability and offer low-level entry requirements. PHP, in particular, has proven to be painless to learn without advanced studies of programming and algorithms. It is now widely used to create dynamic web applications that change according to specific user requests. We shall come back to this later when we discuss the most advanced instantiation of dynamism in web applications, the Rich Internet Applications (RIAs).

It should finally be said that the LAMP software stack is quite old by now, and many of the more advanced web applications are built using a range of other stable and often open-source technologies. Nowadays, programming languages and data storage applications are mixed and matched according to specific needs. Modern web applications are poorly served by 'monocultures' such as the LAMP stack. Polyglot programming (Wampler et al., 2010) has emerged as a new paradigm and claims to target the right tool for the right job, which often leads to less overall code to maintain and also better organisation of code. Modern web applications are heterogeneous and multifaceted, and require the complex composition of different layers of software (Wampler and Clark, 2010).

In all these application designs, resources dominate the World Wide Web. According to the World Wide Web architecture, any resource on the web is characterised by two parts (Webber et al., 2010). First, we need something to represent the resource. This is generally a document describing the content of the resource. So, if the resource is a report on finance, then this document will represent this report. Secondly, we need something to address the resource by. To this end, uniform resource identifiers (URIs) have been set. They give a unique address to anything that can be found on the World Wide Web.

In order to better support the representation of resources, XML (Extensible Markup Language) was added as a web standard (Webber et al., 2010). It offered an evolution of previous ways of computing information on the web. XML is a simplified version of the earlier standard of SGML, which stands for Standard Generalized Markup Language. Just like its predecessor, XML is a meta-language that can be used, for example, by developers to define markup languages as a means to provide an explicit interpretation of texts independently of devices and systems. It allows for a separation of content and appearance, where the appearance of content encoded in XML can be adapted to different systems using a stylesheet encoded, for instance, in XSLT (eXtensible Stylesheet Language Transformation).

The XML example below is taken from the excellent *www.w3schools.com* website, which can be recommended to anyone trying to gain a quick overview of current standard web technologies.

```
<?xml version="1.0"?>
<note>
    <to>Tove</to>
    <from>Jani</from>
    <heading>Reminder</heading>
    <body>Don't forget me this weekend!</body>
</note>
```

The next code fragment is an excerpt from a corresponding XSLT script that selects, for each note element in the XML document, the values of its sub-elements, where the heading is printed in bold and the body is kept within a paragraph. It is quite readable without deeper knowledge of XSLT.

```
<xsl:for-each select="note">
    <span style="font-weight:bold"><xsl:value-of
          select="heading"/></span><br>
    To: <xsl:value-of select="to"/><br>
    From: <xsl:value-of select="from"/><br>
    <p><xsl:value-of select="body"/></p>
</xsl:for-each>
```

From these examples, one can clearly see how content and structure are kept apart using XML and its related technologies. XML is employed for descriptive markup, where the content and markup are held within the same resource. Through the separation of logical structure and content, XML can be used to improve the representation of any resource on the web. The documents to represent the underlying resources can include what is called a self-defining structure. By publishing the schema of the XML definition in another specifically designed language called XML Schema, one can describe exactly how one's own resource is organised. The XML element tags can then be used to add meaning to the content they enclose. All this will help describe resources on the web more accurately. It will support humans in understanding the underlying information, but they might have been able to derive this anyway. XML, however, does more than HTML, as it enables the consumption of the resource by machine agents in digital ecosystems, as we shall discuss later in more detail. But first we return to other technological 'essentials' of the ecosystem.

As discussed earlier, E. Chang and West (2006) offer four 'essences' of a digital ecosystem. It is balanced and self-organised, as well as clustered in domains that are loosely coupled. According to the authors, a range of emerging technologies, from ontologies, knowledge sharing and service-oriented architectures to swarm intelligence, support this kind of digital ecosystem. In the context of digital asset and media management, all these underlying technologies will play a key role. As we have just discussed the XML standard, ontologies and knowledge sharing seem like a good way to start exploring some of the key enabling technologies involved in digital ecosystems. XML is employed to express ontologies.

This book is not an introduction to ontologies, and much more needs to be said about them than can be done in the space of this chapter. One of the most useful sources on ontologies and their use remains Allemang and Hendler (2011). They offer a pragmatic view about ontologies and describe why they support a new level of data and resource integration. According to Allemang and Hendler, ontologies can also be seen as an attempt to formalise the relationship of crowds with their clouds of information and content. They have been around for quite some time now in computing and information science, and they offer a way to formalise concepts and descriptions that are used within an ecosystem of humans and computers. Ontologies provide information to computers and help humans understand the conceptual constraints of their domain. Their aim is to define not just the terms in this community but also their relationships based on a formal vocabulary.

In the context of digital asset management, taxonomies have been around for longer and are still better known (Walter, 2004). They help define relationships between key concepts used in the description of digital assets. In the case of taxonomies, the relationships are limited to hierarchical ones. Ontologies take the idea of taxonomies a step further by allowing any kind of relationship between terms, not just a hierarchical one. In this way, men and women are not just related by being part of the same human species, but can be related in many other more complex relationships.

Ontologies are part of what Berners-Lee has called the philosophical engineering of the web (BCS, 2006) (see also Chapter 4). They help communicate the models we build about our domain. For the digital ecosystem, ontologies establish a language that any member of this ecosystem can use to communicate with any other member, be they human or computer. Ontologies are a communication platform for crowds and enable concept mappings, so that in one part of the ecosystem, communities can call a table a chair, while in other parts, they can keep calling it a table.

However, this communication across concepts is not just linked to one specific digital ecosystem. Ontologies also allow communication with other ecosystems on the web. We shall later discuss how the web is evolving in separate ecosystems led by multinational companies. Ontologies contribute to a more meaningful exchange across these webs. In this context, 'meaningful' implies that information is exchanged so that not just human agents can consume the underlying resources, but also machine agents. It was recognised early on that the future of the web did not lie so much in the consumption of resources by human agents but by that of machine agents. The idea of a digital ecosystem, in which computer and human agents participate side by side and consume together digital resources, was born. The web and its machine agents needed to be able to read the semantics of the underlying information and resources. Tim Berners-Lee called this the 'Semantic Web' (Berners-Lee et al., 2001).

Semantic web technologies and their corresponding service-oriented architectures are the second set of technologies that E. Chang and West (2006) emphasise as building blocks of digital ecosystems. While ontologies claim to be a solution as to how to bridge the disparate languages of computational communities in order to deliver a common communications and meaning platform, web services claim to enable linking of the various computational activities in communities to develop a common technology platform. Service-oriented architectures bring these ideas together into a unified framework.

All computational activities are based on functionalities delivered in various computer languages. Web services offer ways of representing these functionalities on the web, so that they can be understood by any other functionality that might need them. A good example is a temperature sensor on the moon connected via satellite to the World Wide Web. If a weather station needs a comparison between its local temperature and the temperature on the moon, it can ask the moon weather service to deliver its current temperature reading. Two functionalities in a computer network generally communicate via their interfaces, which define points of contact between them. The interface is a point of interaction and a means of communications. Web services generalise this interface concept to the web level. We shall revisit interfaces in our discussion of web APIs later, in Chapter 4.

Web service functionalities can be found by other functionalities in a registry for all web services. The architecture of the digital ecosystem eliminates this central point of organisation, as E. Chang and West (2006) point out, and substitutes it with the idea of collective organisation by distributing intelligence across the web. What they call 'swarm intelligence' is collective intelligence on a more general level, and can take many forms in a digital ecosystem, as we shall see throughout this book. Swarm intelligence is a subset of artificial intelligence and focuses on collective control of organisations, while collective intelligence describes the many forms of collective self-organisation that aim for a solution to any given problem. Both are directly related to the idea of crowds on the web, where members of the crowd work together with a common purpose to make a collectively established right decision. At least for the time being, collective intelligence remains the real source of agency in the digital ecosystem.

For the web, the main working service-oriented architecture is nowadays ReSTful. ReST stands for Representational State Transfer. ReSTful web services are a recent innovation and have triggered a mushrooming of services distributed on the web. ReSTful worked because it kept things simple. Instead of imposing a new framework and infrastructure on the successful web architecture, a new framework was invented that could work with the existing web architecture. Therefore, ReSTful promises to be the 'the architectural style of the Web': 'In many ways, the World Wide Web itself, based on HTTP, can be viewed as a ReST-based architecture' (Elkstein, 2008). Elkstein explains that ReST has taken off as an alternative to previous, more heavyweight attempts to distribute access to services and content across the web. In ReSTful style, a simple network connection is all that is needed, and two examples from Elkstein explain how it is used. Calling from an application or a browser *www.acme.com/phonebook/UserDetails/12345* would deliver phone book entry 12345, while calling *www.acme.com/phonebook/UserDetails/12346* would deliver entry 12346.

Most common web applications such as Twitter or Facebook contain such ReSTful web interfaces that enable access to some of the companies' deeper secrets. Calling *https://twitter.com/search?q=london*, for instance, retrieves all tweets that contain the word 'London'. Finally, to get the same search back in the more computer-readable RSS (Rich Site Summary) format, one can simply use *http://search.twitter.com/search.rss?q=london*.

ReST acts like a postcard in traditional paper distribution of information, which also means that it does not include native security features. These can, however, easily be developed on top of ReST. Sometimes this is forgotten. In 2012, Facebook had a problem securing its own ReSTful interface according to a blog entry by Halliday (2012). Its Midnight Message Delivery App for New Year's wishes was stopped by Facebook after a student was able to read other people's private messages by simply changing the message ID in the URL (Jenkins, 2012).

Not only ReSTful web services have enriched the web experience. Twitter and Facebook are what are called Rich Internet Applications, which behave in a highly adaptable and interactive way, and all from within a browser. In the history of web applications, it was soon found that computation could be distributed, too, if one made not only the servers smarter, but also the clients. The benefits seemed immense. A web user would not have to wait any more for a remote machine to serve their requests but could use their own machine to achieve the same aims. Yet the security concerns also seemed immense. By accessing a remote computer's computational and data resources, one did much more than download documents onto these machines. The early remote computation means of Flash and Applet have never lost these stigmas. While Flash has survived until recently as a format to stream films, Applets are hardly used any more. Even its successor technology, WebStart, has not really broken into the ranks of commercial desktop applications, and remains an exception to the everyday use of the Internet. New forms of Rich Internet Applications are now dominant and, contrary to their predecessors, take most of the computation back to the server side.

Online gaming applications are famous examples of Rich Internet Applications, where complex digital game assets are distributed through the web browsers rather than being preinstalled on an application DVD. At the same time, these rich assets behave towards the user in a highly interactive manner. Next to web services, AJAX (or Asynchronous Javascript And XML) (Garrett, 2005) is one of the key enabling technologies here. It was popularised by Google in 2005 and uses the JavaScript programming language, popular in client-side web development, but enhances it with features that allow it to communicate directly from a client's web browser with the web server who is serving the client's requests. This has made it possible for web applications to act like desktop applications, and not to require Flash or Applet-style intrusions into a user's desktop.

Google mail is one of the more famous examples of these WebTop applications (Web 3.0, 2007), where all that is needed is a browser to run a remote application that behaves almost as well and as quickly as a locally installed email client. In the days before AJAX, users had to fill in a web form and then submit it, before waiting for a server's reply that would update the browser content by uploading a new web page. AJAX does not require a web page to be uploaded each time a user requests a change, which means that the time delay has gone with AJAX and true interactivity on the web has been established. In 2012, Google, together with Samsung, released the popular Chromebook, which completely used the Rich Internet Application stack based on Google's Chrome web browser.

To harmonise the current technology mixtures that dominate the web and enable rich interactivity at the same time, HTML5 will be the new standard for web documents and will allow HTML itself to serve many of the current needs of web applications. It will help define better the inside and the outside of what a browser will support in the future. It introduces new standard markup and reduces the dependency on external application programming interfaces (APIs). For the life of digital assets on the web, the new audio and video elements are particularly relevant. They give content curators on the web a choice of delivery of video and audio formats. HTML5 includes many new multimedia features, especially the new <video>, <audio> and <canvas> elements.

The HTML5 video element, for instance, will play videos or films without the need for developing dedicated plugins. It can be embedded directly in the HTML code and supports multiple sources. This means a video can be in many of the current standard formats from ogg to mp4, etc. Formats are often part of a company's own ecosystem and part of a larger attempt to dominate certain markets, as we shall discuss in more detail in Chapter 4. The introduction of HTML5 has thus also been politically and economically motivated. It is the victory of those who claim universal web standards can deliver on rich interactive web standards and extend the reach of these standards towards the delivery of high-end multimedia content to mobile platforms.

McNamee (2012), in his blog, considers HTML5 to be the next big thing for digital content. It not only enables new content experiences such as 'HD video streaming without a buffer over 3G wireless networks', but also incorporates many of the interactive features seen before only in Flash applications. BI Insider Press agrees that HTML5 might be an alternative to more expensive app development (BI Insider, 2012), and will become particularly important if digital content is to be exploited on the web. McNamee gives the following example in his blog:

> Imagine you are reading David Pogue's technology product review column in the New York Times. Today, the advertising on that page is pretty random. In HTML 5, it will be possible for ads to search the page they are on for relevant content. This would allow the Times to auction the ad space to companies that sell consumer electronics, whose ads could then look at the page, identify the products and then offer them in the ad.
>
> (McNamee, 2012)

HTML5 offers additional functionality to support machine understanding of content and to strengthen its links to other content on the web. Content can be offered because of another evolution of the web: the emergence of the programmable web using web APIs.

Web services and service-oriented architectures have therefore led to a richer Internet experience. But as our short discussion of ReSTful web services has indicated, machines are already better integrated in the web, too, with web services. The real reason why we can speak of a digital ecosystem is because of an idea that extends an old computing principle to the web-scale: application programming interfaces (APIs) (Webber et al., 2010). An API was traditionally used for one computing program to interact with another within a well-defined environment that did not have to be limited to a single computer, but nevertheless most of the time was. Using the ReST innovation and its interpretation of service-oriented architectures, APIs really took off and managed the access to applications online. These applications can be anywhere, as long as they expose their underlying functionalities in a standard way. In this way, products identified in a *New York Times* ad, for example, can come from anywhere in the world.

APIs are a competitive market and split up into functionality and data providers that want to use the web as a platform. They make the web 'programmable' using web services and allow for mashing up of content and services from several sites. According to Yu and Woodard (2009),

Web APIs and mashups are the key components of the global digital ecosystem. To establish these, various registries exist on the web, where all the web APIs are described and put into the context of their use, the most famous of which are programmableweb.com and APIHut. Here, the online crowds can 'share, find, and reuse web APIs'. Thus, they build 'an ecosystem in which people can reuse web APIs and build mashups' (Yu and Woodard, 2009). Web APIs advance the digital ecosystem, the actors of which are now offered possibilities to reconfigure it relatively easily. New applications in the digital ecosystem become a question of (re)composing established applications using their APIs, rather than development.

Blank (2011) ran a survey on a developer site to find out about the challenges the community faces when trying to integrate APIs. The list of complaints about current API services was long, as they are often badly curated. There is little documentation on how they can be used, their interfaces change frequently and maintenance overheads increase with time. However, the survey also showed how closely interlinked the API ecosystem already is. On average, more than five services were integrated, which exceeded the expectations of those conducting the survey.

We have now discussed most of E. Chang and West's key enabling technologies for the digital ecosystem, from the evolution of resource descriptions on the web using ontologies and XML to the development of distributed computational intelligence using web services and APIs. E. Chang and West (2006) finally examine, with self-organising intelligent agents, a more advanced topic that would take us deep into recent research in artificial intelligence. In a highly simplified notion, intelligent computational agents act upon impulses from the environment and derive their actions by relying on a set of rules that have been given to them or that they have learned themselves from past interactions in their environment. They are a key component in contemporary research in artificial intelligence, where agents are supposed to learn that newspapers are not just a source of daily news, but can also be used to kill a fly on the wall, for example. However, this excursion into artificial intelligence takes us too far away from our discussions of digital assets.

Even in the computationally less advanced world of digital assets, we see the beginnings of 'intelligent' digital assets driven by intelligent agents. Crowds and clouds play an important role here. They support the intelligence of the applications and services of digital assets, as well as their distribution across the web. It is key to the concept of (digital) ecosystems that digitally intelligent behaviour can flourish within them.

Adding intelligence: crowds and clouds

In a digital ecosystem, digital assets can behave intelligently, as we shall observe in the various examples throughout this book.

1. Intelligent digital assets know what can be done with them, which means they have a service interface that links them to the functionalities of how they can be used. Digital assets in publishing, for instance, can in this way understand in what kind of publishing workflows they can take part in, as we discussed in Chapter 2. Digital commodities can be sold directly through ads in the *New York Times* and so on.
2. Intelligent digital assets know how they relate to their users and other objects. We have already discussed that ontologies enable a common language in an ecosystem and between ecosystems. Web services do the same for functionalities. Embedding digital assets in ontologies and web services means locating them in the global network of relationships. Their position is mapped for them within the wealth of networks.
3. Once their position is mapped out for them, intelligent digital assets know where they are in the digital ecosystems. They can then, for instance, seamlessly work on the hardware on which they are currently located. They can express themselves whether they are operating on a mobile platform or in a traditional desktop computer environment.

One might rightly object that these kinds of characteristics do not make digital assets intelligent, in terms of how the word is commonly understood. Intelligence in humans is more variable. But our interest is in how digital assets participate in digital ecosystems, and how they organise themselves and relate to the other inhabitants of the digital ecosystem. Then these are elements of their behaviour, which exhibit intelligence, as the efforts of humans and computers are incorporated to allow digital assets to circulate in digital networks. Both crowds and clouds support the addition of intelligence to digital objects and assets. Clouds make their life in the digital ecosystem seamless and enable the kind of processing that computational intelligence requires, while crowds add intelligence where computers fail.

Cloud computing is often misunderstood as something new and big. In reality, it is a much older idea that also targets the smaller needs computer users might have and part of the wider field of utility computing, which provides easy access to all parts of computing resources, from storage to computation. Garfinkel (2011) points out that as such, the ideas of cloud computing are much older than one might think. They go back to the computing pioneer John McCarthy, who said in 1961:

> Computing may someday be organized as a public utility just as the telephone system is a public utility... Each subscriber needs to pay only for the capacity he actually uses... Certain subscribers might offer service to other subscribers... The computer utility could become the basis of a new and important industry.
>
> (McCarthy, quoted in Ivanov, 2009: 37)

This pretty much exactly describes the vision for cloud computing even today.

We have learned to expect to have electricity available as a service whenever we plug an electric device into the power grid. Much like this, cloud computing promises to offer computing resources as a service to anybody interested in using them. They are paid for according to use, just like power from the electricity grid. Cloud computing also promises an elastic service. With higher demand, more resources are available. As long as a user can pay, they can use all the resources they demand. These resources scale seamlessly.

After McCarthy had dreamed up cloud computing, it was finally made possible by advancements in virtualisation technologies (Garfinkel, 2011). Virtualisation is an old technology, as, in essence, all computing is based on some virtualisation and abstraction of resources. The traditional operating system was invented to hide the complexity of the underlying hardware from higher-level programming. A program now just had to ask for something to be displayed on screen without needing to know how this would have to be done for a particular screen model.

Virtualisation in the cloud computing world takes this a step further by abstracting also from the operating systems. Now, if an application asks its operating system to store a file, this can be done anywhere on the cloud and not just on the local machine any more. For the operating system, however, nothing changes, as it can still use the same commands to store the file. The cloud computing virtualisation services, however, will pick up this request and distribute the files according to the cloud computing service agreements. Traditionally, the operating system provides access to the hardware of a system, to various applications on a computer. Cloud technologies are about virtualising these resources, so that the same hardware can be accessed from different operating systems, each of which has their own group of separate applications, which can be utilised on demand.

In the world of cloud computing, the user pays for storage and transfer costs. The latter is measured by the used bandwidth. Unfortunately, even now, most cost models are not harmonised across providers and vary greatly in terms of what is charged and how much for individual activities (Sharma et al., 2012). Taking into consideration the costs, cloud computing is a cheaper alternative for the occasional use of resources and to cover oneself against the odd burst in online activities for which one is responsible. For longer-term use, cloud computing costs are still often higher than using in-house services (Buyya et al., 2009), but this situation is evolving fast.

If we consider cloud computing to be part of utility computing, access to cloud resources is principally organised in three dimensions (Garfinkel, 2011):

1. Infrastructure-as-a-service: This is the classic cloud idea and offers access to storage or computational resources. Amazon S3's large-scale online storage infrastructure (Armbrust et al., 2010) is the example for this; more commonly known nowadays is the Dropbox online file storage system.
2. Platform-as-a-service: Here, the user is offered a platform for their own services. A good example is Google's API engine (Lenk et al., 2009), which can be used to deploy code quickly online (Wang et al., 2010). A user does not have to worry about keeping the server environment up to date. But the crowd also has such services, with Amazon's Mechanical Turk platform being the most prominent one (Ipeirotis, 2010).
3. Software-as-a-service: Here, whole systems are no longer administered in house, but outsourced instead. A commonly used example is Google's Gmail service, which allows users and companies to use Google's email services online rather than having to set up their own email servers.

Infrastructure-as-a-service is maybe less known in the professional digital asset and media management world, as it happens on a deeper level of technological integration. The user has full control and freedom over applications, as it looks like the extended version of one's own computer. Users can run any software they want. In order to use a platform, they generally have to comply with certain software requirements. They are, for instance, limited in the programming languages they can use or the functionalities of the underlying infrastructure they can address. But they have full control over the applications they develop, and they can exploit their surplus in any way they want to.

Better known in the digital asset and media management world is software-as-a-service. Within this model, the freedom to install anything is given up upon in return for easy-to-use and safe applications offered by third party providers. There are many digital asset management applications that run as software-as-a-service, and it will very likely be the most commonly associated cloud service for digital asset management. The popular Widen Media Collective solution, for instance, is a fully cloud-based software-as-a-service solution that supports mainly high-use but low unit-value digital assets in marketing (Widen, 2012). Finally, for a book on emerging digital ecosystems, platform-as-a-service is most likely an important model, which has only just begun to develop its impact in digital asset management. Platforms are provided upon which developers can deploy their own services, but, with the right tools, general users can, too. A simple example might be a web deployment service that allows developers to put their code online more effectively and efficiently. Here, we also find our crowds next to the cloud services, as we shall discuss later.

All of these service dimensions have led to big business by now. According to Gartner (Columbus, 2013), infrastructure-as-a-service will achieve a compound annual growth rate (CAGR) of 41.3 per cent from 2011 until 2016, and constituted in 2010 already a market of about US$3 billion. Software-as-a-service will grow at a steady CAGR of 19.5 per cent from 2011 until 2016 from a larger basis US$34 billion in 2010. The largest investment gain will be seen for platform-as-a-service, with 27.7 per cent. In short, cloud computing is not only already big business, but will be even bigger in the near future.

Originally, a main business motivation for cloud computing was to stop losing out on business opportunities, because the necessary computing resources were not idle. Amazon found that its book-selling servers were often running at only 10 per cent capacity, just so they could cater for peak times such as Christmas sales (Hof, 2006). Amazon therefore decided to offer its spare server capacities to others and developed a new business, claiming that it would make information technologies for others easier. These others can now transfer the responsibilities of running the systems to people specialised in this task and most often this will come at a lower cost than was originally anticipated. However, at the same time, by handing over the responsibilities, one also gives away control. Cloud computing services are very hard fought over at the moment, because most vendors would expect that customers would stay with them, once they have made an initial decision in favour of them.

Recently, and with heightened media attention, cloud computing has come under scrutiny as to whether it really delivers all the benefits it promises. Breakdown of services, loss of data in the Amazon cloud, inability to connect or, even worse, breakdown of trust and malicious attacks on user profiles (for example, in the Sony gaming cloud) remain a problem and get worldwide news coverage. Many legal issues are also still unresolved in this new field of computing. The European Parliament (Nielsen, 2013), for instance, warned in the beginning of 2013 that using cloud resources in the USA for data storage might allow US officials to read this data on request. Later in 2013, the Snowden debacle confirmed their worst fears.

Interesting, more personal cases include the questions of who inherits digital assets accumulated in the cloud if the original owner dies, or how the heirs get access to the assets in the cloud. Contrary to some media reports, Bruce Willis did not sue Apple in 2012 over iTunes inheritance (Wittaker, 2012), but many feel he should have disputed a digital content contract with Apple, which gives users only unlimited rental of their bought digital content, rather than ultimate usage rights.

For those concerned about handing their data to big outsiders, next to the known publicly available clouds such as Google, Apple or Amazon, private cloud providers are delivering software to deploy a cloud infrastructure within an enterprise. OpenNebula and Eucalyptus are examples, and have been used successfully to deploy clouds for science communities. OpenNebula was developed in a European Union-funded project called RESERVOIR, and has the authority of the CERN data centres behind it (Darrow, 2012b). Such private and public clouds do not need to exclude each other. In the emerging ecosystems that use clouds, we shall see a mixture, where private clouds are deployed to deal with the common services and tasks in an enterprise, while public cloud services from providers such as Amazon or Google will be used for the occasional bursts.

By now, we are in the middle of an openly battled struggle over supremacy in the cloud space, which is fought using means of the digital ecosystem of APIs as well as service and content lock-ins. What has dramatically been called the Amazon API battle (Darrow, 2012a) is the struggle over whether the deep parts of the cloud infrastructures are open to users as well, or locked behind commercial and proprietary APIs, such as the Amazon Cloud and Microsoft's cloud-computing platform Azure.

Simply cloning these APIs does not really mean cloud computing, Lew Moorman has claimed (Darrow, 2012a). He is president of Rackspace, the world's second largest cloud hosting firm after Amazon. These APIs hide the deep technology use and undergo the original promise of virtualisation that any operating system can run on any hardware. Furthermore, proprietary clouds might use their own file formats for digital assets, which makes it difficult to customise one's own digital asset management solution.

We have only recently seen the beginnings of a new open cloud infrastructure and open-source alternatives to commercial providers such as OpenNebula and Eucalyptus. These may never have the same breakthrough as other open-source technologies like the Linux operating system. It might well be that security requirements and high availability demands make open clouds impossible. But even within the commercial alternatives, there are huge differences in terms of openness and interoperability. Apple famously made its iCloud offering completely private. It solves the problems of syncing digital media assets across Apple devices, but concentrates on Apple devices. The integration of this backup and replication solution into the Apple apps is very deep, but it is difficult to access any other tools and services beyond Apple's own.

Apple's cloud is therefore single-minded, and the company's assumption is that the cloud will really matter to the masses where it solves specific problems like the exchange of digital content across various media devices. In this sense, it is a different and much more limited idea of a cloud than McCarthy's original concepts. It is by far not a ubiquitous utility like the electricity grid. Apple's iCloud therefore seems incomparable with other companies, like Amazon Web Services' cloud platforms discussed earlier. A comparison between Amazon and Google's efforts is here more enlightening.

Hinchcliffe (2008) demonstrates that Google's idea of integration of its own cloud system goes much further than Amazon's and well beyond the simple connections via APIs. To a degree, both Amazon and Google offer relatively open systems. On its machines, Amazon lets a user install whatever they wish, while Google commits itself to various open software development tools, such as the programming language Python, to help deploy dynamic and scalable runtime applications quickly. For Amazon, however, client capabilities are more or less disabled; the cloud computing services provide computing machines through their APIs, as just discussed.

Both architectural designs are optimised towards a diversified marketing market, where digital assets can be offered on a subscription basis (Hinchcliffe, 2008). Both Google's and Amazon's ideas offer distinct possibilities of the development of digital asset management technologies, and one can therefore assume that the growth of digital asset management and cloud computing will go hand in hand.

While large-scale enterprises still use the cloud mainly in smaller dedicated applications but keep their own enterprise-scale solutions in house, the cloud has been taken up by companies that build their business models on the web platform and need something to support their twenty-four-hour availability demands. The most prominent user of Amazon's cloud computing infrastructure is therefore with Netflix, one of the biggest digital asset and media companies in the world.

Netflix is one of the world's largest on-demand web streaming digital media companies, famous for its home film and TV services, and another example how cloud computing enables the digital economy in the age of big data and big content. The Netflix Tech Blog (2010) names Netflix's reasons for using Amazon's cloud offerings as follows:

1. Outsourcing the data infrastructure to Amazon helps focus Netflix's development efforts on improving its services.
2. Cloud architectures help deal with surprises in customer growth numbers.
3. Cloud computing is simply the future of online digital media, as it requires new advanced services and 24-hour availability, 365 days a year.

Unfortunately, for Netflix this exact availability is not always given and not all of those 365 days are equal. During Christmas 2012, a major outage at Amazon meant that Netflix users had no films for Christmas (McMillan, 2012). But cloud computing is the future for Netflix, because this helps the company to build a better and smarter digital media experience for its customers. It can focus on new services that help users find and enjoy the right digital assets for them, as we shall discuss in Chapter 4.

IBM is already one step ahead in making computing smarter through the cloud, and has released its smarter computing initiative. It hopes to trigger the next-generation use of assets, from power grids to traffic management. In this IBM plan, cloud computing is used to connect people and integrate software solutions in new and unforeseen ways. IBM's Smarter Cities initiative (Harrison et al., 2010), for instance, links city communities and their volunteers with computing power, to try to predict where the next crisis will happen, or where the next robbery will take place, as promised in a famous TV ad for IBM's smarter cities work. Whether digital predictions will really become this sophisticated can be seriously doubted; it may well be a marketing exaggeration. What is interesting here, however, is the fact that human intelligence and community intelligence are seen as integral parts to make the planet smarter using the cloud.

The Amazon Web Services' architecture (Hinchcliffe, 2008) recognises the same fact that a smarter planet does not mean substituting human with computing intelligence, but integrating the two together. For Amazon, not only computers but also humans provide intelligence in the cloud, because the organisation allocates its Mechanical Turk service to plug into collective intelligence right next to its other cloud computing services according to the analysis of Hinchcliffe (2008). In the Google architecture, this kind of service is completely missing; but then again, Google has always trusted artificial intelligence first. The crowds have failed in helping to set up its core search service, and user feedback on the relevance of website was for a long time banned by Google. Only recently has Google changed its strategy and put more trust into the crowds again, sourcing knowledge from them in its new Google+ services, etc. Amazon, on the other hand, has always had good experiences in terms of crowds supporting the sale and consumption of its digital assets by providing recommendations to one another. It has a long history of crowdsourcing book descriptions and recommendations on all its products.

Working the crowd

As Amazon has shown, crowds really play a role on the web when their intelligence is sourced to improve products and services. According to Howe (2006), crowdsourcing is a neologism that combines the crowds with outsourcing. The idea is to use crowds to add value to one's (digital) assets. The Oxford English Dictionary is one of the first examples of using volunteers to enhance the knowledge output. Volunteers were already in the late nineteenth century being asked to go through books and note down key words in their context. According to Howe (2006), some of the contemporary key principles of crowdsourcing optimise the results that one can expect, if one relies on the crowd. The crowd needs to be dispersed. This will help get the most out of the highly distributed knowledge in the world. Crowdsourcing aims to connect specialists. It does not matter whether these specialists are amateurs or not, or whether they know a lot about highly popular fields such as military history or genealogy, or whether they inhabit the long tail of knowledge like, for example, the history of water plants in the English midlands. If the crowd is dispersed, we can trust it to find the best stuff.

With crowdsourcing, we use the ecosystem to connect brains not computers. Where the computer fails, ubiquitous human computing (Zittrain, 2008) sets in. Many examples have now been established on the web, so users often do not even notice that they take part in crowdsourcing. In the reCAPTCHA application (Von Ahn et al., 2008), for instance, the crowds help digitise books when they are actually trying to enter websites or fill in forms in order to purchase items from the web. ReCAPTCHA is deployed as a barrier to stop spam-bots from automatically activating forms. Most Internet users will have used reCAPTCHA, but probably without realising that they are participating in crowdsourcing.

Galaxy Zoo (Lintott et al., 2008) is an example for a crowdsourcing application that encourages crowds to engage actively with science. It is among the most famous science applications in crowdsourcing, where galaxies are classified according to their shapes. The human brain is far better equipped for this task than any computer shape recognition software. The project has been so successful that by now, Galaxy Zoo is running out of galaxies to classify.

Galaxy Zoo has been so popular that we now have a whole host of follow-on applications. For instance, Galaxy Zoo's team, together with the UK's Met Office, runs Old Weather (Oomen and Aroyo, 2011), an application to help research climate change. Here, ship logs from the First World War are analysed by volunteers to find weather recordings, which should help with developing a comprehensive overview of the historical development of temperatures since the early twentieth century.

One of the earliest scientific volunteer computing projects was SETI@home (Search for Extra-terrestrial Intelligence) (D. P. Anderson et al., 2002), which used volunteers' computing power to analyse radio signals in order to help search for extra-terrestrial intelligence. It runs on the BOINC infrastructure (Berkeley Open Infrastructure for Network Computing) (D. P. Anderson, 2004), which will be discussed in a little more detail here, as it demonstrates some of the most importance features of many crowdsourcing applications.

The BOINC platform contains, among other things, a credit system service that assigns credits to volunteers after completing tasks. It contains highly customisable workflow mechanisms that allow experts to be integrated easily into the computation, in order to review task results. Priorities can be assigned to particular jobs, depending on the number of volunteers. Finally, websites can be built quickly and released with all the necessary functionalities to launch a crowdsourcing project. Especially important seems to be that volunteers have online facilities to communicate their results with each other and compare outcomes of their task work. In some BOINC applications, monthly prize draws are included.

Next to science tasks, crowdsourcing applications are by now very common in the heritage sector. In the world of heritage computing, further factors make the crowd popular. Here, crowds function as a cheap workforce and supporters of the museum brand. Funds are generally sparse in the heritage world, so utilising community knowledge becomes a necessity in ambitious projects to add value to one's own heritage assets. But this is often not the only motivation. Involving the dispersed crowd also emphasises the importance of a museum's holdings (Holley, 2010). Once museum objects are discoverable online, they may also tempt people to visit the museum offline again, to see the objects in real life. Furthermore, the public might develop a sense of common ownership. All these developments took place in one of the most successful heritage crowdsourcing project: the digitisation of the Australian newspaper archives. In 2007, the National Library of Australia began to digitise out-of-copyright newspapers. It used crowds to help correct OCR (optical character recognition) mistakes, and the public followed in large numbers and analysed millions of lines of text (Holley, 2010).

However, dispersed crowds can help more than cultural and scientific causes. They also serve business, as they are an essential part of developing its services. The most famous example is the already cited Mechanical Turk, part of Amazon Web Services (Ipeirotis, 2010). It is not based on volunteer contributions, but each participant gets paid a small amount per each task completed. In Amazon's terminology, these are Human Intelligence Tasks (HITs), and requesters define tasks and upload data, while workers (aka Turkers) do tasks and get paid. Typical tasks include the identification of email addresses in texts or the labelling of images.

The Mechanical Turk is aptly named after a device in the seventeenth century that made history by pretending to be the first chess automaton. In truth, the automaton was a very small man hidden in a box below a chessboard, hidden from view by mirrors. The real miracle was that the small man was a better chess player than all but a few of his opponents. In any case, the name of a human pretending to be a machine is well chosen, as Amazon sees its Mechanical Turk as being on the same level as its web services. As is common for its other cloud services, Amazon provides services to link any application into the Mechanical Turk crowd. Just a few scripts allow requesters to manage and direct the crowd directly from their applications.

A good example for the use of the Mechanical Turk crowd platform is the LabelMe application, as described by Sorokin and Forsyth (2008). It helps train computers in the difficult task of classifying objects in an image by building training image databases for computer vision. While scientifically the project has been a success, some HIT workers complained that it was a lot of work for little money. As research by Ross et al. (2010) shows, average wages for Mechanical Turk workers are less than $2 per hour. Originally, most HIT workers came from the USA, but nowadays most are from India and many consider the online work to be an essential part of their work life, to help sustain their livelihood. We shall discuss exploitation of the crowd in more detail in Chapter 6.

Crowdsourcing should therefore be seen not as the opposite of computational services, but as their logical continuation. Should you have ever read computer science and listened to descriptions of service-oriented computing, a tutor might have given you the challenge in the first class to develop a service that makes coffee. The obvious solution, once you have understood that you can plug into distributed human intelligence with a service, too, is to create a service that will send an email to someone in charge of coffee and ask for fresh coffee. Crowds are just different nodes in the platforms and offer a very specific service, powered by human brains and, in the case of the coffee, some minor muscle, too. You just have to make them work.

Crowdsourcing as a service is already a common phenomenon on the web. Ushahidi (Okolloh, 2009), for instance, is an open-source (mobile) response platform, which employs the principles of dispersed crowds for emergency response and other applications. During the immediate aftermath of the earthquake in Haiti, Ushahidi helped connect volunteers on the ground with remote experts in centralised emergency response units. Again, the trend is towards not just a single application, but a platform that makes it easy to connect to experts on the ground equipped with mobile phones. Countless other projects are now run on the Ushahidi platform, and it is seriously considered by the United Nations as a tool for disaster prevention and management.

Stringfly (2013) is an example for applications that make crowds-as-a-service a fully commercial tool. It is an app for Android and Apple platforms that allows users to earn money if they give brands useful information from the ground. Users might also function as citizen reporters to report on contemporary events that affect brands. In this way, a photograph with a cola can in front of Big Ben or a spontaneous report on a beer-drinking competition in a local pub might make money for mobile phone users.

Applications such as Stringfly or Ushahidi rely on the fact that the crowd is embedded in the real world and can be contacted anywhere. These applications would have not been possible without the more widespread (mobile) broadband that connects the crowds wherever they are. Digital media delivery platforms and devices have advanced immensely since mobile broadband technologies have emerged that support a seamless big content experience for users. With broadband, the volume of information on the web could rise to unseen levels, perhaps by 20–30 per cent every year. Though the information load becomes larger and larger every year, it is also delivered at much greater speed and much more targeted. In the broadband-driven mobile ecosystem, we get it all and all our digital media needs are served anywhere and any time – or so we might think, at least.

In this mobile ecosystem, we are all connected through digital objects. They are, next to fellow users of these objects and algorithms to manipulate them, the only thing we shall ever meet in the mobile ecosystem. The mobile media ecosystem, as discussed by Feijóo et al. (2009), has enabled digital content to be sent seamlessly between digital devices. Digital content knows how to behave, whether it is displayed on the small screen of a mobile device or on the larger screen of a home computer. The niches of our existence and every interest we have that makes us distinct have become inhabited by digital objects, which we are ubiquitously connected with and can choose to make our own.

In order to support our new big digital media needs and desires stemming from the big data pipes of broadband technologies, new data infrastructures have been developed, together with new methodologies to access data assets through them. These are generally summarised under the name NoSQL (Not only Structured Query Language) (Sadalage and Fowler, 2012). SQL has been the dominant standard for databases for more than 30 years. It allows users to query databases using a specifically designed query language and concentrates on relational databases (Sadalage and Fowler, 2012). Whether the data problem was big or small, and whatever the format of the underlying data, relational databases have been de facto dominating the market for all needs.

This SQL dominance goes so far that users interested in implementing a digital asset management system will generally call their repositories 'databases', though they have little in common with these relational databases. The latter are, generally speaking, optimised towards structured data, while most digital asset management applications focus on unstructured information such as media assets, as discussed in Chapter 2.

In the world of social digital media, new applications have evolved and more flexibility is required to represent data assets and express their relationships (Robles, 2012). With the emergence of social media applications and new digital content, data stores for the web have progressed, and the NoSQL movement has gained lots of traction and speed, especially in various cloud-based models. NoSQL is closely linked to the evolution of data clouds (Sadalage and Fowler, 2012), which we shall investigate in more detail in Chapter 5. More famous example implementations of NoSQL databases then also come from the known providers of cloud computing, as we shall discuss.

There is more flexibility now in the choice of schemas and formats that make these new types of data stores work with complex aggregated digital assets so well, as they are common in the digital ecosystem. The ecosystem has plenty of formats just to store the same video assets, lots of annotations based on these and additionally has seen many metadata standards come and go. One of the latest hypes are the polyglot persistence data infrastructures (Sadalage and Fowler, 2012), which aim to combine the best of the established technologies of relational databases with new types of NoSQL databases. Often digital asset management systems are already designed to support polyglot persistence, without calling it such. It is common for the catalogue to be stored in a relational database, while the actual assets are stored in data stores more suited towards large digital objects. Different user needs are addressed by different parts of the system. Polyglot persistence gives this established behaviour a name, and in this way helps with its understanding. But it also allows people to separate the several parts of the system better in order to address new user needs by providing easy access, for instance, to social relationships.

E. Redmond et al. (2012) describe one such digital media application for a traditional digital music and band application. A simple key-value store is used as a cache for ingested data, but also to support queries that require direct access via a set of keys to a set of digital media objects. In this way, it is easy to find all tracks by an artist, for example. A document database, specially designed for storing XML documents, is the general source of reference for all band data and artist information, and keeps the data in sync across the whole data ecosystem. Most interestingly, however, special attention is given to relationships by creating a graph database to store relationships between artists and their music assets or the crowds that support the digital music processes.

Graph databases are based on the more flexible Euler's graph model, with nodes and edges between them, and all the standard well-established means of graph processing. Graph databases are thus quite an old idea (Angles and Gutierrez, 2008), but only since the advent of the social web has there been a renewed interest in developing them into full-scale storage infrastructures. They scale well towards complexity or towards information that is not uniform (Eifrem, 2009), and relationship queries such as the band member relationships perform much better than in traditional databases. In this way, it becomes easier to track an artist across different bands that they might have participated in. Digital media is put into the context of its production and use by crowds. The more connections digital media can find, the better. It demands access to all other digital media on the web and wants them to be as open as possible.

The next chapter will discuss how open ecosystems evolve and how they end up in a system where not only the digital objects are open but also the means to link them, a promise of the open linked data movement. It fulfils what Tim Berners-Lee, known as the inventor of the web, has heralded as the third evolution of the web (MacManus, 2007): the Giant Global Graph (GGG). The first evolution formed the Internet as a network of machines, while the second was the World Wide Web protocol, designed to exchange documents (in HTML) across the Internet, mainly between humans. The third will be able to qualify the links between people and 'the things these documents are about' (Berners-Lee, 2007). This will help unlock untapped assets hidden in enterprise documents, which were estimated to be worth US$3 trillion in 2005 (Bergman, 2005).

Tim Berners-Lee believes the Giant Global Graph will become particularly important in the context of the mobile ecosystem, where users with their mobile devices will be embedded in an environment of digital and non-digital things, and the websites as representations of these things will disappear behind the direct concern for them. The World Wide Web behaves like a global file system, but the Internet as a GGG becomes more concerned with how the browser can become the centre of how crowds interact with the world itself. 'Browsers that were a mere window to the world may become a real wide entrance to the world itself' (Web 3.0, 2007), if the ecosystems become fully open.

This chapter has concentrated on the technologies and methodologies that have made digital ecosystems possible. We discussed the evolution of the web into something where humans and machines can both feel at home. Machines especially had to do some catching up in terms of employing some new effective means of machine communication on the web. Machines made good use of the web once it had become ReSTFul, with open APIs making web services accessible. Web services and APIs have allowed crowds and clouds to settle fully into the web and demonstrate their ability to deal with its content. Their real strength comes from scaling along with the increase of the web's content, as we shall see in the next chapter, when open content in open ecosystems threatens to unleash a tsunami of data.

4

Open and closed digital asset ecosystems

Abstract: An absolute must for the engagement of crowds and clouds is that content and, if possible, applications are open, as we analyse here. However, again digital ecosystems add another dimension to these discussions. In order to develop profits based on the web, the future web will entail a combination of open and closed pieces of infrastructure and content, which raises the question of whether this undermines its original promises and will therefore lead to its demise. Digital ecosystems seem to offer not just a way for companies to profit from the web while staying open, but also a way for us to understand these developments.

This chapter takes us through some of the corresponding debates from open data in sciences and governments to the question of effective use, which is sometimes forgotten. If we consider effective use, we need to include open infrastructures in our debates on open data, which we see as one of the main motivations behind open linked data. Otherwise, filter bubbles and walled gardens develop, and, as we shall see, these walls are difficult to tear down.

Key words: open and closed digital ecosystems, open access, effective use, walled gardens, filters, architecture of participation, linked data.

Open content and its effective use

We have already discussed how digital assets are one of the cornerstones of the emerging global digital network of people and things. In order to take this position, however, digital assets need to be open to be deployable to various environments, as seen in the previous chapters. In Chapter 2, for instance, we noted the World Economic Forum (2007) see real new value developing only if the digital ecosystem is as open as possible.

This chapter continues this discussion by investigating what it means to be open in this context, and whether and how this might stand in contradiction to the idea of valuable assets for a particular organisation. Here, we would like to concentrate on understanding open and closed digital ecosystems, and where asset value might stem from if we consider either option – i.e. how asset value can be developed in the completely open environment as envisioned by the World Economic Forum in comparison to closed systems that only allow particular users the right to use the assets. This will include discussing not only web APIs again, as a means of opening data and services, but also how open data leads to potentially uncontrollable amounts of information that need to be filtered.

Some might consider the idea of valuable assets to contradict the idea of open digital ecosystems, as organisations might want to protect this value and give away as little as possible (Newfield, 2013). At the same time, we have said that value is always realised in the consumption by others. The less closed a digital environment is, the easier it will be to realise this consumption. The Internet has been such a success as it has made it easy for content to be published for general access and consumption. It uses open protocols such as HTTP and URIs (uniform resource identifiers). Only with additional effort is content not open once published on the web. So, it seems logical to start from the idea of open content and work backwards to understand how we can close it, and why we might want to do so.

Recently, the debate on open access to material and open material itself has gained new momentum (Nariani and Fernandez, 2012; Yiotis, 2013). Since the beginning of the commercial use of the web, its tendency towards open content, which it inherited from its early days as an instrument of global scholarly exchange, has concerned many observers and participants. But only since digital assets have started to play such an important role in the web, and more and more are transferred on the web for distribution and publication, has the debate on open content heated up. In the earlier days of the commercial exploitation of the web, digital content itself was more another way of distributing physical assets. The Amazon shopping basket contained books, which were posted to consumer households. Now, next to these books, we find digital books, digital films, etc. in shopping baskets. This has become possible due to better networks and improved digital productions. The variations in what we buy online has changed the perception of open content. Now, the openness of the content needs to be problematised and protected.

When discussing heavily loaded terms, it can be useful to start from a particular strong advocacy position, because from here the differences between the involved parties can become much clearer. Also, one will often find here the most developed thoughts, with people dedicating much of their intellectual life to the position they defend. This does not make the position necessarily right, but helpful to develop an understanding. In this sense, a commonly used definition of open content comes from the non-governmental pressure group Open Knowledge Foundation: 'A piece of content or data is open if anyone is free to use, reuse, and redistribute it – subject only, at most, to the requirement to attribute and share-alike' (Open Knowledge Foundation, 2011). This definition links the value of open content to its use and reuse. Only if this use and reuse is free can the value be accessed easily. The second part of the definition refers to copyright questions, which we shall ignore in this chapter, because there are lots of interesting investigations elsewhere; for one in the context of content industries, refer to Lemley (2011), for example. The Open Knowledge Foundation goes on to specify that open content includes access at a minimal cost, which ideally means that the content can be freely downloaded from the Internet. Once the content has changed hands, one should be able to redistribute it freely, reuse and modify it 'under the same terms as the original'.

Another heavily cited source in the debate on open content is Peter Suber, Director of the Harvard Office for Scholarly Communication. He concentrates on barriers for open content (Suber, 2010). For him, there are mainly two barriers: financial or 'price' barriers; and legal and technical barriers, combined as 'permission' barriers. This makes sense, as technical barriers are often marginal in the decision to make content open. It can be that content can only be accessed and used within a certain environment that is not generally accessible, but even then the challenge would rather be to make this environment more widely accessible. Essentially, open content is challenged by financial and legal barriers, driven by the interest in closing content, while the technical barriers are a derivation of these financial and legal barriers. Digital ecosystems are one of these technical inventions intended to open or close digital content.

The move towards open content is often driven by those areas that have a certain moral obligation to commit to openness, because not they but the public have financed the creation of content. For years now, those in the sciences have debated heavily the pros and cons of open sciences, not just because most are still publicly funded, but also because they claim that sciences contribute to the advancement of human knowledge as a whole without limits. Their data, the results of science, therefore belong to humanity. This information should be open. On the other hand, science is also based on the existing volume of knowledge, which is, in many parts of science, predominantly digital by now. Limitations on access and reuse of information therefore stand against the advancement of sciences as such. This is the background for the recent actions of scientists against Elsevier, which was reputed to put profits before scientific progress and enclose scientific knowledge in publications (Gowers, 2012).

The same reasoning is behind recent government policies for science publications. The Finch Report discussed how research articles could be published via open access in the UK. The Working Group on Expanding Access to Published Research Findings, chaired by Janet Finch, concluded that for the 'Gold Route' for open access in scholarly publications, authors pay publishers to get their research published. The publications themselves would be free and open (Finch Group Report, 2012).

In the Finch world, open science leads to 'big science'. If all scientific knowledge becomes available at the click of a mouse button, the data and information background of sciences becomes big. According to Hey et al. (2009), we are in a fourth era of science, a fourth paradigm, where science is driven by an ocean of zeroes and ones. In the first era of science, experiments guided the generation of new knowledge. In the second era, it was the theory, while the third has seen the large-scale expansion of knowledge by simulating natural environments. The fourth paradigm heralds new data-driven science based on open data resources.

Whatever one might think about these classifications, it seems clear that there is an increasingly important area in sciences that is dependent on discovering patterns in large amounts of data. In order not to miss out on any patterns, this data has to be open. Data-intensive scientific discovery is not possible without open data. The value of scientific assets is therefore directly related to their reuse by other scientists. The digital assets are part of the scientific communication and function as a recording of past knowledge upon which future knowledge can expand. Openness is therefore a necessary condition of scientific value.

A second area where open content already dominates the debates is government data. Here, openness is part of the drive for political transparency in democracies. The public good is quoted to get governments to publish all their data so that citizens can participate and understand processes of power. Data.gov.uk is the UK site to collect and publish all government digital assets (Shadbolt et al., 2012). As of 2012, this website had thousands of data sets, released with open standards and an open licence. It has managed to establish an active community of data users and developers, and has led to many spin-offs, including crime tracking apps and traffic mapping environments.

Data.gov.uk has many sibling sites in other states or local authorities, which all commit to the notion of open public data. The site is just one of its kind. By now, many data marketplaces can be found on the web. They range from commercial to open communities. Examples include:

- large-scale public data sets such as the Amazon Public Data Sets (*http://aws.amazon.com/publicdatasets*) or data sets extracted from Wikipedia (*http://wikipedia.org*);
- community efforts such as Freebase (*www.freebase.com*), with mainly data on people, places and things, or the DataHub for many different kinds of data (*http://datahub.io*);
- many subject-specific sites like OpenStreetMap (*www.openstreetmap.org*) with user-contributed mapping data or Global Health Facts (*http://kff.org/globaldata*); and
- emerging commercial platforms of for-sale data sets such as infochimps (*www.infochimps.com*), which contains many data sets on social media in its marketplace. Interesting here is also the recent Microsoft effort to build a Windows Azure Marketplace (*http://datamarket.azure.com*), which aggregates 'a wide range of content from authoritative commercial and public sources in a single marketplace' (Flasko, 2010). Amazon has similar offerings.

Returning to public data and its places, a UK government report (HM Government, 2012) describes 'public data' as 'the objective, factual, non-personal data on which public services run and are assessed, and on which policy decisions are based, or which is collected or generated in the course of public service delivery'. The first public data principle also implies here the use of data either in business or the public sphere.

Therefore, it needs to be published with open standards (just like the open science data) and through a single point of access, which is the data.gov.uk portal. Public bodies are further encouraged to publish inventories of their data. The current UK government expects, from its commitment to open data, a culture change in the public sector if data sets are always considered to be public at some point. This should help improve the transparency of government decisions, which should in turn lead to better trust in government by the public.

Governmental open data will come from all divisions of the government that publish their data into a central repository (a platform) – a government data cloud, so to speak. Developer crowds then work on apps, information visualisation applications or other types of computational use of the government data cloud. Finally, digital citizens can use these apps and visualisations to inform themselves quickly about their government's activities or to get involved with local activities. The idea is for local communities to get involved directly with the data that affects them. How many crimes are committed in my area? How much money has been spent on my local playground? How are these decisions made? The previous UK Labour government has linked open data directly to big data and promised at the time to 'unleash a tsunami of data' (Rogers, 2010), which would let citizens participate in the decision process and help kick-start business by offering lots of data to work with.

Both open science and open government therefore define open content via its use value for others. However, there are limitations to this definition of openness as usefulness. We see two principal limitations. Firstly, the definition of value as use value goes too far, as financial obstacles are at least partly ignored. In both e-government and open science, the assumption is that value might only be realised if the environment is open. However, they both define value solely by its use either in other science or in the general public. Considering Suber's descriptions of the obstacles of open data, and the financial barriers towards its adoption, this view on value as use value seems limited. Even in scientific data, significant financial value might hide. Here, biosciences, where data is freely available, compare to chemistry information (abstracts, patents, physical data), that constitutes a multi-billion dollar business. Chemical Abstracts (ACS), Beilstein (Elsevier) and Wiley are the major players. Open data for chemistry or biosciences means a loss of revenue, which universities in turn could then invest in their research. We could quote again the famous toothbrush comparison from Chapter 2, that 'biologists would rather share their toothbrush than share a gene name' (Pearson, 2001).

The second limitation of equating value with use value is that the definition of value as use value does not go far enough if use is understood only in an abstract way, which we want to discuss next. We discuss two problems of 'effective use'. On the one hand, users might not have the means to exploit open data, and on the other hand, there might be too much data for them to use it effectively. They might drown in the tsunami of open data.

To understand open data use better, Mike Gurstein, editor of the *Journal of Community Informatics*, introduces the idea of effective use and claims that open data based on a reduced concept of use can help cement existing inequalities rather than lead to an improvement in public services. With 'effective use' (Gurstein, 2003), he describes the distinction between the opportunities provided by new technological means and the possible realisation of these. Then, computing students in Stanford may find completely different realisation possibilities for their ideas than students in contemporary Kabul. Everyone might have access to open data, but 'not everyone has access to the digital infrastructure, to the hardware or software, or to the financial or educational resources/skills which would allow for the effective use of data or any other digital resource' (Gurstein, 2011). These inequalities are generally summarised as the digital divide, and it is good to remind ourselves of it in the context of digital ecosystems. Gurstein emphasises that open data is provided not just by opening the access to data, but also by considering effective use.

To understand issues in the social position of the online crowds, community informatics deals with the 'application of information and communication technology (ICT) to enable and empower community processes' (Gurstein, 2007: 11). The insights of community informatics on effective use are, however, often ignored in the debate around open content (Davies, 2010b). Open data sets aside the question of whether open information can equally openly be exploited and consumed:

> There would, in this context, appear to be some confusion as between movements to enhance citizen access to data and the related issues concerning enhancing citizen use of this data as part, for example, of interventions concerning public policies and programs.
>
> (Gurstein, 2011)

As an example, Gurstein cites work by Benjamin et al. (2007) that has investigated the use of digitised land records in Bangalore. The authors look through the stories that provided evidence for use of the Bangalore land records since they have been opened on the web. The evidence they have collected shows that those with 'means to use the digital infrastructure, those from the upper and middle classes, were able to exploit the new information to expand their own land holdings at the expense of the lower classes' (Gurstein, 2011). The upper classes also had the capital to exploit the open land records, as they had access to the skills necessary to make effective use of them.

We could translate Gurstein's thoughts on how digital divide develops even from the digitally well-meant openness agenda into our question of the relationship between humans and computers in the digital ecosystem (Davies, 2010b). The advancement of humans should not be forgotten if one considers the development of digital ecosystems. Gurstein (2011) himself cites, as a counter-example to the land records in Bangalore, the attempts by Community Advocates in Solano County in California to use the California Health Interview Survey (CHIS) (California Health Interview Survey, 2010). Here, the human factor is not forgotten, as the community activists could use not just the freely available data but also the freely available training on how to use this data. Admittedly, the example of health records in a developed country does not compare well with the examples of land records in the developing world. Nevertheless, it shows the principle of how the human can be recognised as an important factor in the open ecosystem of digital assets such as land or health records. In the cited example, it is the emphasis on including the training needs of participants that has helped develop effective use. Solana County Community Advocates were trained to make effective use of the data assets provided by the CHIS for their community needs.

In an online comment to Gurstein's article on the social issues behind open data, Tim Davies (2010a) points to his own investigation of the problems within the UK's open data movement, which he has developed in his dissertation (Davies, 2010b). He directly links the focus on the technicalities of open data such as the emphasis of machine-readable open data to the ignorance for other factors that hinder open data's effective use. He asks for an 'equality architecture'. We are not sure whether we would follow Davies's point that a technology focus might lead to ignoring social issues, as this sounds deterministic. However, it seems to us that the concept of digital ecosystems includes an equal emphasis on crowds and clouds, on human and machine factors. In this sense, it is an 'equality architecture'. This kind of architecture is actually included in the thinking of most proponents of open data. As seen, at least the Open Knowledge Foundation includes effective use in its definition. Thus, we think that Davies and (partly at least) also Gurstein both address the wrong people with their demands, as they concentrate on convincing the open content movement.

The story about Bangladesh has shown that one needs to be careful not to confuse the term 'open' with 'good' – an equation that is sometimes made without thinking through what open actually refers to. Open data has value in so far as it is a member of the digital ecosystem and the digital ecosystem itself is open, which would allow the general public in Bangladesh to have the same means of exploiting open data as the already privileged landowners. However, when open content could be leading to unintended consequences, whether it might harm communities rather than benefit them is a question that is not often asked, simply because the proponents and opponents of open content often either completely affirm open content or simply reject it. It can be counterproductive when it is not used within an open ecosystem that includes equal participation rights and possibilities for all actors. This would include human and machine actors.

To be fair, the advocates of open data and open content we cited earlier, such as the Open Knowledge Foundation or Suber, would include effective use in their demands. For them, open data also includes the drive towards opening silos of data with open technologies at the same time, that can work with anybody's digital infrastructure and include anyone's skills. This is called the open linked data movement and demands open ecosystems and infrastructures next to open content, which is the technical realisation of the equality architecture.

An equality architecture can be achieved if open or even semi-open content is kept interoperable, which is why there are significant efforts, from those in the arts and the sciences to those in the government, to harmonise the data output. Standards are here really a way of providing cost-effectiveness. For the rest of the chapter, we shall discuss ways of making content publicly available in increasingly standard-compliant ways so that it can contribute to the equality infrastructure that Davies demands. We start with how the web is transformed into walled gardens and how these can be broken up using web APIs. We finish with opening up not just the data, but also its access completely, and investigate the progress made in the open linked data world. One can see 'open linked data' as the final logical consequence of the attempts to open up content.

Closed environments and walled gardens

As discussed in the previous chapter, HTML (the standard language in which the web exchanges documents) is one of the greatest success stories of open participation, precisely because it opened the web to the participation of not just a few chosen ones (aka developers and computing experts), but all ordinary web users. Participating on the lowest level is as easy as writing a Word document, saving it in HTML and putting it online. The by now famous Web 2.0 is simply the radical continuation of this ease of publishing digital content on the web. Tim Berners-Lee has always said that blogs and wikis and other Web 2.0 applications are just easy ways to create HTML documents for the crowds: 'If Web 2.0 for you is blogs and wikis, then that is people to people. But that was what the Web was supposed to be all along' (Berners-Lee, quoted in Andersen, 2007: 5). Tim O'Reilly, heralded as the inventor of Web 2.0, agrees with Berners-Lee (O'Reilly, 2004). He goes as far as to identify the open Web 2.0 with an 'architecture of participation' that advances the original idea of the web.

Effective use of the web does not, however, stem simply from putting stuff out there, but from 'linking' it: 'More germane to my argument here, the fundamental architecture of hyperlinking ensures that the value of the web is created by its users' (Gurstein, 2011). Value is again use value and created by users. For O'Reilly (2004), linking and sharing increases the value, because it leads to distribution of one's information and one's digital content. 'There's an implicit architecture of participation, a built-in ethic of cooperation, in which the service acts primarily as an intelligent broker, connecting the edges to each other and harnessing the power of the users themselves' (O'Reilly, 2007: 22).

But there are always attempts to break down this general use value of the web as an architecture of participation into smaller pieces. O'Reilly uses his idea of an architecture of participation to criticise Apple's attempts to monopolise and Balkanise the web by limiting the linking: 'There's only a limited architecture of participation in iTunes' (O'Reilly, 2007: 34). For him, there are three ways to build up digital content for the web. For the first one, he quotes Yahoo's way of creating a web directory by paying people to do it. When the Web 2.0 was invented, the open software community had impressively shown another way of building digital content. The open-source system Linux was built by the contribution of many software assets by volunteers from around the world. For O'Reilly, however, the real example for the architecture of participation is the original Napster. Here, a user contributed digital content while downloading it, thereby adding value to a large virtual content store. As a user adds content without interrupting their activity, 'participation is intrinsic to Napster, part of its fundamental architecture' (O'Reilly, 2005). While Napster is about radical participation in the use value of the web, Apple attempts to define the use value solely in terms its own content and services. Here, the digital ecosystem is about creating new islands in the web and walling off information.

The inventors of the web meant it to be universal and neutral, which implies that it should be able to run on any kind of hardware, using any kind of software. Net neutrality means that communications cannot be restricted for political or commercial reasons. For many, these building blocks of the web are under threat. Recently, Tim Berners-Lee warned that the Internet is under attack, as net neutrality comes under fire from political and economic interests, and as we shall see, most of these interests are about digital content:

> Some of its most successful inhabitants have begun to chip away at its principles. Large social-networking sites are walling off information posted by their users from the rest of the Web. Wireless Internet providers are being tempted to slow traffic to sites with which they have not made deals. Governments – totalitarian and democratic alike – are monitoring people's online habits, endangering important human rights.
>
> (Berners-Lee, 2010: 80)

Berners-Lee here introduces the idea of 'walled gardens' and warns that the web could be broken into 'fragmented islands'. We have already learned about a similar metaphor that draws open data against data silos, but it is clear that Berners-Lee goes a step further than just technical and legal issues generally covered in the discussion on open data.

Interestingly enough, most of Berners-Lee's examples for attempts to create fragmented islands stem from the world of digital content and its effective reuse. He cites a cable television company that invested in their own broadband networks only to restrict the use of content from other television companies via their broadband. Social media companies such as Facebook and LinkedIn create user profile data and add information about a user's activity on their site in order to offer value-added services that users, advertisers and so on are willing to pay for. But they limit this data to their own sites. Again, it is the content that is 'walled off'. It cannot be accessed separately beyond the ecosystems of Facebook and

LinkedIn. Apple is a master in this, as it even uses its own protocols to enable access to and downloading of content. iTunes, probably one of the biggest digital asset and media management systems in the world (if not the biggest), lets users download content not via the open Internet HTTP protocol, but the proprietary protocol of 'itunes:'. This is why O'Reilly sees Apple as one of the main culprits that breaks the architecture of participation (O'Reilly, 2004).

One of the most recent analyses of the 'state of Apple's ecosystem lock-in' comes from the blog of Alexander Hoffmann (2012). Eaton et al. (2011) had previously investigated the antagonisms Apple was involved in to realise its digital ecosystem at the tension of 'control and generativity'. Hoffmann (2012) first compares the Apple ecosystem attempts to wall its gardens off with more traditional strategies employed in other industries. He gives the examples of car manufacturers forcing customers to buy specialised parts that can only be found by special subcontractors. He also cites the attempts by digital asset management industries to bind users to their own digital media assets by employing digital rights management or formats that can only be opened in customised environments.

With his reference to the wider world of lockdown of media assets, Hoffmann points to the fact that walling off an ecosystem is often justified using factors beyond the control of individual companies. Apple, for instance, might rightfully claim that it offers digital asset owners a controlled environment where misuse of their assets is excluded. While the iPhone is its earliest example of a universal mobile consumption platform, with iTunes, Apple controls its digital assets:

> Apple's iPhone not only acts as a phone, but also acts as a personal navigation device, an e-book reader, a personal game device, and a personal medical diagnostic device among other things... It is Apple who creates the device, operating system, and iTunes store that enables creation and delivery of digital content and apps.
>
> (Eaton et al., 2011: 1)

Only a small amount of the assets in iTunes come from Apple; most are by outside providers. With iTunes, Apple provides them with the secure environment in which to share these. Apple can point towards the digital asset providers for potentially controversial definitions of 'misuse'. It can claim that it disallows the advertisement of pornographic products in its ecosystem, in order to protect those who want to sell and use digital products for children, etc. iTunes enables this protection.

Hoffmann rightly emphasises that the lock-in of Apple's ecosystem is all about digital content, from whatever side you might look at it:

> This kind of ecosystem lock-in essentially doesn't allow the customer to take the content and move to another ecosystem/platform. There's another kind of ecosystem lock-in – or lock-out for that matter – which sometimes goes hand in hand with the first one: prohibiting the user to (easily) consume content that originated from a different source/ecosystem.
>
> (Hoffmann, 2012)

Both ways of locking content in and out have essentially the same effect of protecting digital assets. Apple is happy for software engineers to develop apps for the ecosystem, while Facebook, as another example discussed in Chapter 2, sees itself as a platform that invites contributions of code and functionalities. Both, however, lock away their digital content. Apple is different from Facebook, as, for the time being at least, the latter does not have dedicated devices such as iPhone, iPods, etc. But the rumour goes that Facebook is working on this, and the already discussed Facebook Home App might be the first step.

Hoffmann goes on to analyse various types of digital media assets and how they are walled off in the Apple ecosystem. Apple's iTunes is at the centre of its efforts here. Digital music is the first kind of digital asset, traded on a large scale by Apple via iTunes. A specific feature here is the interplay of digital asset management stores (iTunes) with dedicated hardware, which is in this case the iPod, and the revolution it enabled in the music market. Nowadays, digital music in iTunes is free of DRM (digital rights management) limitations and stored in the standardised file format (Hoffmann, 2012). This implies that digital music content as an established digital asset is relatively open in the Apple ecosystem, and can be played and consumed on multiplicities of platforms. This contrasts with the current situation for digital video, which is fully DRM-protected. Digital videos can be imported into the Apple ecosystem by using file conversion tools, but digital videos bought on iTunes cannot be played outside of Apple devices or those that are strictly controlled by Apple ecosystem software. Eaton et al. (2011) provide us with an analysis of how Apple's struggle with Adobe over the Flash standard finally led to Apple's control of the video offerings in its ecosystem.

The situation is similar for Apple digital books, which have recently become the most traded digital asset. E-books bought within the Apple ecosystem cannot be read outside of it. But in the case of e-books, Apple does not limit the access to the digital ecosystem for distributors of e-books, as long as they are willing to develop apps that help users read these books. They thus sit, in terms of lock-in, between digital music and digital videos. Amazon's Kindle app is a good example, but Apple also supports the ePub standard and Adobe's PDF through various custom-built applications. For Eaton et al. (2011), publishers ignored the demand for e-books in the Apple ecosystem until it was too late, when Apple had already established its dominance. Hoffmann (2012) completes his list of digital assets with podcasts, which can be freely distributed to other ecosystems, and software applications in general (such as games), which can only be used within the Apple ecosystem.

As one can see from Hoffmann's analysis, the distinctions on what a closed digital ecosystem might look like compared to an open one are not as clear-cut as one might think. It all depends. According to the business strategy for various digital assets, Apple uses a mixture of open or closed formats and usage restrictions to build its ecosystem around iTunes. Furthermore, one can probably understand, from Apple's attempts to unlock music while locking video, where Apple's current business interests lie. The advent of the iPad has brought about a new focus on digital videos and new forms of distributing them, using apps that are not part of the traditional web.

Other companies make their money mainly from exploiting digital content that can be openly found on this traditional web. Because it has emerged as the main entry point for the web, Google has an interest in as much as possible happening on its site. Sergey Brin, Google's co-founder, has therefore criticised in several interviews (Barnett, 2012; Katz, 2012) the tight control of Google's competitors on their data and the walling-off of the digital content from the web. In an interview with the *Guardian* (Katz, 2012), Brin said that the open web is under threat not only by censorship through governments, but also by commercial attempts to lock in content and other services. But Brin wants his comments to be understood not as a direct criticism of Apple et al. directly, rather as a defence of the open web, as he makes clear in his own profile page on Google+: 'Lastly in the interview came the subject of digital ecosystems that are not as open as the web itself... To clarify, I certainly do not think this issue is on a par with government based censorship' (Brin, 2012). He believes that the Internet has been a great force for good and has enabled, with its free flow of information, political freedom.

The co-founder of Google has consequently been criticised for being hypocritical. He is the co-founder of another big company that tries to create its own digital ecosystem, which also tries to wall off its own data and information. However, bearing in mind his comments on the background of Berners-Lee's ideas for an open web, Google can rightly point to its attempts to largely adhere to open web standards. In particular, Google has been one of the main contributors to the growth of open web APIs, which we shall discuss next.

O'Reilly's architecture of participation in the Web 2.0 world is finally enabled by the web APIs, as discussed in Chapter 3. These allow users to climb the garden walls and access the digital content and services behind them. Web APIs have become famous, as many well-known providers of digital content on the web have developed simple means of accessing their content behind their publicly available websites. This includes the largest web-centric companies like Amazon and Google, where the latter in particular has produced many widely used web APIs such as the Google Maps API. This allows web users to embed Google Maps into websites.

Yu and Woodard (2009) have shown that the remarkable growth in the use of APIs is mainly due to the highly interconnected use of a few major ones such as Google Maps. But recently we have also seen newcomers quickly gaining an astonishing market share. The *New York Times*, for instance, provides a web API to access its vast amount of articles, while in the UK the *Guardian* newspaper has an established API to access its archives (Aitamurto and Lewis, 2013). Both are now intensively reused across different digital ecosystems.

Why do companies allow access to their deep content secrets? The Google Maps API success should already give a good indication that the content value can multiply through linking. All of a sudden, Google content is deeply entangled with many high-profile applications around the world. Its content is delivered not just through its own services but freely through the services of others, too. The programmable web allows for a much deeper integration than the traditional one of one's own services into the web cloud. Google Maps is a service that many high-profile web applications cannot do without any more.

Beyond Google Maps, web APIs hold particular promises for the digital asset management world, as they enable secure delivery of digital content. In a typical hypothetical scenario from brand management, Global.com, a multinational global delivery service, wants to control the look and feel of its brand's logos very closely. Global.com has therefore decided that it wants its outlets not to store the logos on their own servers, but rather to access them from a central digital asset management repository. They can be downloaded for use in online and offline publications via a web API. The local and national outlets of

Global.com can access the logos by embedding a small piece of software into their websites and digital publishing solutions, which ensures that, via a web API, the latest version of a logo is delivered in a timely manner.

In general, a web API is a way to retrieve and also keep updated digital content on a remote web location. In our scenario, it is probably unrealistic to assume a case where the local outlets would need write access to the brand asset management system. The web API for its logos gives Global.com a way to keep its brand media assets separated from the local implementations of a website. The content is delivered by means of a web service. In general, web services, as explained in Chapter 3, are used to implement web APIs. There are then ways of securing access to the digital content as well, but this require too much complicated technical detail for the time being.

Both web APIs and architecture of participation include strong commitments to sharing content via the web and an open ecosystem based on it. They are ways of loosely coupling content and services via the web. If one wants content to be deeply embedded in a client's software, then it is better to hardcode the content into it and deliver it with the applications itself. The Apple logo in the iTunes store app, for instance, will be downloaded with the app itself. If one has no interest in sharing, one should simply stay away from web APIs altogether.

In the theories of Web 2.0, communities benefit from having all the content on the web available. They build up collective intelligence using it. However, for a long time there has been concern about how much we can consume in terms of information, which was earlier defined as the second area that inhibits effective use. As the term 'data tsunami' implies, open content can also be too much. It does not necessarily lead to a better understanding of the content. With quantity, the quality of data might suffer; a problem that is not really solved at the moment, even with the crowd's collective intelligence. While the proponents of the web point to the power of the crowds and Wikipedia, opponents can point to the problems of the blogosphere and the madness of the masses, as recently seen when the crowd went into a brutal witch hunt after the Boston bombings from 2013 (BBC, 2013). Even if data is of high quality in the first place, one can also observe a general unwillingness to ensure that this data stays of high quality. If data is taken care of more carefully, it might spread across the web, with different copies overlapping in information and being of different qualities.

These considerations lead us directly to another problem with the tsunami of information unleashed by open data. It can simply be too much to extract any kind of meaningful information from it. Even the current amount of closely peer-reviewed scholarly information is too large for any single person to consume and digest (Wikipedia, 2013d). But it is not just the information quality that might suffer from the ease in which publishing is done on the web; the technical quality might also be lacking. It is too easy to publish in formats such as HTML or PDF, which are not the best ones in terms of reusing data. Open data sets often come with complex processing requirements and require lots of investment on the side of those who want to consume them (Davies, 2010b). They are in effect offloading financial investment into their reuse onto the (re)user, because complicated standards make it necessary to pay for advanced means to import and use the content behind them.

Faced with the tsunami of information and the costs of consuming this information, we let others help us with making the decision on what to consume. Readers might think of Google as the great entry point to all the information and how it might control our view on it by delivering ranked lists of relevant content for our searches. But we have witnessed another almost unnoticed revolution in the mass organisation of information in recent years. It is based on a technology that is as old as information retrieval applications such as Google: filters. Web APIs allow for the publishing of online content that can be consumed by other machines or humans. They push out and publish their information to many remote places at the same time. The consumption is then often aided by filters, which help the consumer to decide what is relevant to them.

Filters are complementary to search engines (Baeza-Yates and Ribeiro-Neto, 1999). Search engines try to deliver digital content to dynamic user queries from a large relatively stable repository of digital content. Filters assume a stable query and a dynamic set of content. So, for instance, a particular filter program gives you the chance every evening to access films online that correspond to a particular taste in classic westerns. We have entered the now ubiquitous world of recommenders, which are essentially filter applications, with the exception that they often learn about the preferences of users from past behaviour rather than ask users to set these preferences.

We discussed earlier collective intelligence as a new way to organise the web according to communities. There is also the other more computational side of collective intelligence, which requires computer support to help with decisions. 'Recommender systems' use complicated statistical algorithms to build models of consumer behaviour (Resnick and Varian, 1997). They generally use information from the items under consideration, the past behaviour of the existing user, as well as other context information about related users and items. They mix all these as features in a statistical calculation and deliver a prediction on what might be relevant and of interest to consumers.

Principally, there are two ways of doing this (Alag and MacManus, 2009). The first one is an item-to-item comparison. To represent items, we use their descriptions to establish statistically what kinds of similarities to descriptions of other items exist. A second approach to build recommender systems uses the descriptions of item users to establish items that similar users might prefer. The first approach therefore compares the content, while the second one compares the tastes. A model for taste is based on features. In this sense, if one user is from the same town as another user, the first user might also like a history book about this town that the second user bought. Most of these recommender activities are based on long-established computational methods to calculate similarities between texts/descriptions. They work well and include large computational cluster (or clouds) to achieve the highest satisfaction, while at the same time providing effective computation.

In this computational collective intelligence environment, the more the better. The more information the recommender has collected on past behaviour of the users, the more information it has about a particular item and its related items, the better its model of the future needs and its predictions. The better-known recommender systems operate on millions of items. Amazon's recommender system, for instance, is based on working out an item-to-item matrix that counts the number of users who bought item X and also bought item Y. Then, the recommender will suggest item Y to another user who has just bought item X. This is simple but highly effective, and scales well with millions of items and users.

In another example from digital media management, the online film company Netflix has tried to make statisticians and computer scientists rich (Bell and Koren, 2007). In 2006, it offered a price of US$1 million to anybody who could deliver an improvement to their existing recommender algorithm Cinematch or, as a *Telegraph* article from 2012 put it, to those, who could read the minds of users best (Williams, 2012). As a resource, Netflix provided 100 million ratings, information on 480,000 users and 17,770 films, as well as six years of data from 2000 to 2005 inclusive. A few winning teams shared the prize. Those who won recognised that not all users are equal in front of the recommender systems, and that they need to be classified carefully. For instance, some film genres are more geared towards female audiences, while others are generally watched by men. An equally important factor seems to be whether films are rented on a Monday morning or on a Saturday night. Identifying these relevant aspects lies at the heart of the success of successful predictions and filtering.

Filtering is key to the success of businesses in the global digital ecosystem. The current struggle for dominance in the ecosystem is also one for who can best read the minds of users by accumulating as much knowledge as possible on their behaviours. For Netflix and Google, this has meant trusting less in what people tell them they would like to see and relying more on what their algorithms tell them the users would like to see, according to the complex matrix of user behaviour and descriptions of things out there. The challenge, however, quickly becomes how to show something new, something that none of the people associated with oneself has seen before or even thought of. The 'new' often does not compute, and traditional statistics cannot necessarily find it either, as one of the best introductions to data sciences argues (Janert, 2010). This standard introduction ends by stating the obvious fact that is often forgotten when faced with the tables and graphs that statistical analysis produces: 'The most important things in life can't be measured' (Janert, 2010: 434).

Big money is currently flowing into building filters for online content, but much less thought is spent on how to help users escape from their nearest neighbours in the information and content space. The problem of breaking out of filters has been labelled the 'filter bubble' (Pariser, 2011). Alternative strategies currently include asking friends and other users for new recommendations, and therefore relying on human imagination and collective intelligence. Whether this is workable and will deliver different results remains to be seen.

The 'filter bubble' has become a major concern in the digital economy and society. The term was first used by online activist Eli Pariser (2011) to express how algorithms determine nowadays what we can see of the web's content. These algorithms carry the great promise of delivering to us only the information in which we are interested. In order to do so, they develop models of one's interests and tastes. These have allowed Netflix, for example, to interest its users in more of its content and to sell more of its digital assets, as it presents more digital content to its users that agrees with their viewpoints. However, the danger is that a filter bubble develops around the user, in which conflicting viewpoints disappear. Pariser uses his own contemporary example of searching Google for British Petroleum (BP). A simple experiment with his friends revealed that googling for BP can deliver 'strikingly different' results.

Depending on one's past searches, one might see at the top either the latest investment opportunities for BP, or news stories describing the Deep Water Horizon catastrophe. Pariser believes that this leaves us alone with our own 'invisible autopropaganda', as the *Economist* (2011) argues.

Because the filter bubble is about realising collective intelligence by filtering, it is rather less related to the above-discussed concern of Berners-Lee about web silos and islands. Pariser expresses more disbelief about how the information on the web is divided top-down by algorithms, and his arguments are similar to those who criticise the ranking of Google as too focused on certain content and avoiding a non-mainstream view. We need to put the idea of a filter bubble into the context of what we know about the relationship of filtering and searching, and how both are based on the same or sufficiently similar algorithms. Then, Google does present, at some point in its rankings, everything it can find about an item. It is for the user to go through this ranking and pick out the information they need. In this sense, the filter does not take away information from users. Pariser's friends could have obtained the same information on British Petroleum if they had gone far enough down the rankings. They just need to know about this and behave accordingly.

There are other criticisms of Pariser and in particular his ideas of how Facebook limits his political consumption (Homo Luddite, 2011). There are also suggestions on how to overcome the filter bubble, which are closely related to our viewpoint of the digital ecosystem as the art of combining human and machine labour. The filtering algorithms of large social networking sites ensure that online crowds are connected in the platforms they inhabit. In order to trust the links they are exposed to, these crowds want to understand where the links come from and how they can be changed. They demand that the links between the assets and their relationships with other assets and all digital things will be open, too. In this way, an equality architecture is realised based on open environments.

Open environments

We have learned from the Google experience that people do not trust algorithms designed by large corporations with their own dedicated commercial interests to make decisions for them. The dilemma is clearly that on the one hand, we want digital content to be open, but on the other hand, once it is open and anyone can publish it, there is a question of how to make it effectively usable by everyone. As there is so much content, we need the support of powerful algorithms to help us filter it. The next step is therefore to open up not just the digital content, but the digital technologies that support it, too. People mistrust Google because it conceals how it generates links to other sites. An opening up of these links would tear down the walls around its garden and would indeed lead to open knowledge in the crowds. Adding to open content the promise of open methods of generating and linking this content is the promise of open linked data (Bizer et al., 2009).

Linked data is the evolution of the evolution of the World Wide Web. Tim Berners-Lee (2007) reflected that the original web concentrates too easily on just one type of digital content. The original web is about documents, but most members of the crowd want to address much more – they want to address things: media objects and things hidden in texts such as places and purchases, etc. To distinguish these, Berners-Lee concluded that the web needed to evolve first and learn 'computational semantics'. For him, the next great challenge is to create a meaningful web that can be understood by all actors in it, humans and computers. The semantic web, as he has called it (Berners-Lee et al., 2001), realises this vision of a web where content and services are freely shared among machines and humans. It is based not just on open content but on open knowledge, too.

The semantic web as an evolution of the original web has never really started. It has promised to interlink open services and has developed relatively complex standards and mechanisms to publish services and make them understand each other. The web ecosystem participants were not able to accommodate these. Linked data is the semantic web done right (Glaser and Millard, 2009) and evolves it, as it concentrates on getting the simple things done right first.

Linked data is based on the use of uniform resource identifiers (URIs), part of the standard web world, to represent 'digital things' and the relations between them (Bizer et al., 2009). Berners-Lee (2006) summarises how to represent resources such as digital content and services, relate them and discover information about them. The four principles are as follows:

1. Use URIs as names for things.
2. Use HTTP URIs so that people can look up those names.
3. When someone looks up a URI, provide useful information, using the standards.

4. Include links to other URIs, so that they can discover more things.

URIs are the standard way of pointing to things on the web. URLs (uniform resource locators) are their better-known cousins and locate things or, in web terminology, dereference them. If one types a URL into a web browser bar, then that location's information will be retrieved. URLs are therefore also URIs, but URIs can also use other conventions to name and address things. For instance, ISBN numbers identify specific books. HTTP is, as explained earlier, the standard transfer protocol on a web. The third point Tim Berners-Lee refers to is the assumption that linked data will make information on the web machine-readable. To this end, he refers to the Resource Description Framework (RDF) standard. In a text jointly authored with Tom Heath and Christian Bizer, he explains the need for RDF:

> Whilst HTML provides a means to structure and link documents on the Web, RDF provides a generic, graph-based data model with which to structure and link data that describes things in the world. The RDF model encodes data in the form of subject, predicate, object triples. The subject and object of a triple are both URIs that each identify a resource, or a URI and a string literal, respectively. The predicate specifies how the subject and object are related, and is also represented by a URI.
>
> (Bizer et al., 2009: 3)

Linked data and the semantic web split up the world of knowledge not into documents, but into these triples, which can be encoded in the RDF format. These are basic statements that relate a subject of a statement with a predicate using a relation. Each relation takes the form subject-relation-object. Let us assume we have two traditional documents on the web. The first one states that 'Houses with gardens are popular in London', the second one that 'London is the capital of the United Kingdom'. We could extract the following statements as subject-predicate-object from two documents:

house has garden
houses are-popular-in London
London is-capital-of United Kingdom

Please note that there are, of course, many more such statements derived from the documents. These are just examples where we used names such as London as short versions of a URI that uniquely identifies them. The point here is that London is now a qualified link between the information in the first document and that in the second. We now know that houses with gardens are popular in the capital of the United Kingdom. The linked data space makes concepts into links.

Only Berners-Lee's fourth principle makes it truly linked data by using concepts as links. In the current web, documents are interlinked with hyperlinks. This technique has proven to be immensely successful. However, these links cannot be semantically enriched. The grand vision of linked data is to create large repositories of such triplified statements and to use these either to browse all the information on the web by following the implicit links in triples, or to deliver information such as that about houses with garden in the UK capital directly to human and computer agents. We could combine the two documents above, as we assumed that the 'name' London (identified by a URI) is unique and in both documents identifies the same thing (in this case, a place). The linked data ecosystem is the overall joint space that is spanned by all the possible triples (statements) that one can make from all web resources. Human and computer agents alike can use this knowledge to navigate and understand all the available information.

This global knowledge space is founded in these triplified data sets, which means we fall back on an old philosophical idea about how to structure the world in subjects, predicates and objects. In a less well-known interview, Tim Berners-Lee stated that the web seen this way is 'now philosophical engineering' (BCS, 2006). He elaborates on the idea that it emerges from a few simple principles and web scientists can create systems. Triples have a lot to do with how philosophical systems wanted to describe the world. For triples, the cell in a data table represents the simple atoms of which the world consists. Each triple corresponds to a cell in one gigantic table of things/facts. These facts are brought together if they are considered to be the same – and they are, if they are addressed by the same URI. Instead of documents, things are referenced.

As this book might be read by librarians, it is important to note that linked data is not simply another metadata format. It is data and only in so far as metadata itself is data. One can publish metadata as linked data, as, for instance, in the Europeana collaboration, which is a European Cultural Heritage aggregator, and link it to data such as full-text documents on the web (Heath and Bizer, 2011). Very exciting, from an information science point of view, is the elimination of the distinction between metadata and data that linked data promises, at the end of which stands the global data web or the Giant Global Graph that we presented earlier. This also means that assets such as complex multimedia files, which can only be described in metadata, are now naturally part of the same ecosystem as web documents, which can be indexed by search engines.

Linked data is about publishing structured information using the web as a platform. It reuses the web's well-organised means to address information (URIs) and gives meaning to the links by allowing a formal definition of the relationship. Recently, we have seen linked data being extended to media assets that dominate digital asset management. The BBC, for instance, uses linked data principles to retrieve data from community sites such as MusicBrainz for their own digital music sites. This partly goes back to research described by Kobilarov et al. (2009), which analyses how BBC programme data is published using open linked data principles in order to overcome self-contained microsites that could describe one programme correctly, but not its links to other programmes.

The aim was to embed this information directly in the HTML programme pages on the BBC website rather than externally via specifically designed APIs. Kobilarov et al. (2009) showed that it is possible to use open linked data to cross-reference facts and things in legacy systems and provide context to BBC programmes by referencing outside digital music assets not owned by the BBC. They used the de-facto hub for concepts in the open linked data cloud, DBPedia's serialisation of Wikipedia content (Auer et al., 2007), in order to establish semantically meaningful links between digital media items and their programme descriptions. In this way a 'concept ecosystem' (Kobilarov et al., 2009) develops, centred around DBPedia. Kobilarov et al. finally present how text mining techniques are used to extract concepts from BBC documents in order to provide these links, moving away from a 'language of tagging', as is currently common in digital asset management, towards a 'language of linking' (Kobilarov et al., 2009).

Concept extraction is also at the centre of research done at the Salzburg NewMediaLab, together with Red Bull, to enhance their digital media assets with contextual information using linked data. To this end, a Linked Media Framework was experimented with by Schaffert et al. (2012), which attempts to answer the challenging question of what links between digital media objects could look like. While links are by now commonplace in the world of textual documents and can be enriched with triples, it is far more difficult to understand how media such as video and its fragments can be interlinked. As was the case with the BBC, often the 'media surroundings' (Kurz et al., 2012), such as title or subtitle of an image, are used instead of the content of the image.

The aim of the research in Salzburg was to try out linked media approaches in the real-life context of the Red Bull media asset management system. According to Kurz et al. (2012), the Red Bull Content Pool (*www.redbullcontentpool.com/content/international*) is the central repository of media content related to the many sports events organised by Red Bull. It contains mostly videos that Red Bull promotes to other media publishers for reuse in their broadcasts. Next to the video, the repository contains further annotations such as the location of the event, as well as transcripts of the videos. It is this additional information that can be used to enhance the retrieval of the Red Bull multimedia assets by extracting Red Bull thesaurus concept terms from it. In summary, for the Red Bull Content Pool, linked data:

- enhances the existing metadata with outside links to, for example, DBPedia;
- publishes the digital media assets in a way that they can be reused more easily by outside media outlets; and
- offers the potential to embed the Red Bull digital media deeply in the cross-references of the global web (Schaffert et al., 2012).

All these are essential to gain network value, which we shall discuss in Chapter 6.

This chapter has discussed the condition without which there would be no digital ecosystem. It needs to be open in some way, in order to let services and data move around freely. This implies that its content needs to be open for (re)use. As seen, it is open science and open government data where this idea of reuse has especially become pertinent. Here, most of the current experiments with open data take place. However, what makes the digital ecosystem idea so interesting for digital content and other participants in the global network is that it also provides a means of closure. We have analysed this in detail for the Apple ecosystem, where it has become clear that 'the tension between control and generativity lies at the heart of the digital ecosystem innovation' (Eaton et al., 2011: 3).

At the same time, open does not automatically equate to good, and we need to consider effective use. Use of open data is effective if not just the data is open but also it comes with open means to exploit it. O'Reilly has called this an architecture of participation, where content resources are freely and equally shared. However, open data with an architecture of participation can also become too much. We need effective algorithms for filtering the open data tsunami to get relevant information. These filters are by now the main first points of content with open content on the web for anyone, which threatens to cause a filter bubble, where we only see the kind of content these algorithms are intended to permit us to see. Open linked data promises to allow for effective use and to work against the filter bubble, as in its world, we are also in charge of the infrastructure for publishing and consuming digital content. This is particularly vital as open data quickly develops into big data, where we really need to control the means of analysing and consuming it.

5

Big data collecting

Abstract: Crowds and clouds contribute to what many consider to be the next big thing, as they support the analysis of big data, and their combination is itself an answer to how big data challenges current computing infrastructures. Once understood from the perspective of crowds and clouds, big data or big content becomes one of the main drivers for the change we are describing. Digital ecosystems are, in many ways, set up to deal with big data and make it work as an economic force for change.

This chapter first attempts to define big data from its use. Big data is much older than current debates might suggest. Science data has been big for a long time and has also driven the innovation of new ecosystems that could make this big data work. Today, many big data challenges are still driven by the demands of extreme science, but also by other big data organisations in business and government. The chapter investigates mainly social media applications and some of the current limitations of applying big data analytics here, before concluding with some critical remarks regarding the Big Brother potential behind big data.

Key words: data, information, knowledge, big data, datafication, social media, Big Brother, big data poor.

Big data and digital ecosystems: theories and models

In this book, we have often mentioned big data. In the introduction, we discussed how the rise of crowds and clouds is directly linked to the recent focus on big data and challenges of processing it. In Chapter 4, we continued this discussion with an analysis of how open data leads to big data that might flood us with information – the 'tsunami of information'. Crowds and clouds offer countermeasures here. This chapter provides a more in-depth investigation of big data based on a distinction between content and data. Crowds are presented as those helping collect big data, while clouds offer methods of storing these collections in new and unforeseen ways. Without the redevelopment of our digital environment through clouds and crowds into a digital ecosystem, the era of big data would not have been possible.

In order to address big data from a digital asset and media management perspective, we need to take a step back and discuss the relationship between content and data once more. We said in Chapter 2 that big data is big content, because, for instance, in medicine, big data is mainly linked to the amount of video data now available for research. In Chapter 2, we also argued that crowds and clouds work best where they add intelligence to the content, so that it becomes readable and processable by computers. We needed to add semantics to content in order to make this processing possible.

As previously discussed, semantics in computing does not directly provide meaning, as in everyday language, but limits the number of interpretations of a given syntax by using formalisms a computer can process (Kahn et al., 2009). Consequently, there is already a potential tension that needs to be understood before we can proceed to find out what this has to do with big data. If semantics enables reuse by machines, and computational semantics is about limiting interpretations, then in order to enable this reuse, we sometimes need to break out of these limitations. We simply do not know enough about potential reuse in order to define the right semantics clearly, which is why, in big data, we often need to go back to raw data. As we shall see later in this chapter, big data technologies are designed to do exactly this – at least in parts. This chapter therefore discusses how we advance from digital media and content, and make it data for machine consumption.

Adding semantics to content is one way to turn content into data. In information science, one of the most fundamental distinctions is that between data, information and knowledge. This distinction is not perfect, as Zins (2007) points out. There is, for instance, often the imagination of a hierarchy between the three concepts, where information follows data and is followed by knowledge. However, we also know that there might be knowledge where we have no data, while information and data are often used as synonyms in everyday language. Tuomi (1999) even argues that data should be higher in the hierarchy than knowledge, as data only emerges after we have information. Finally, Dretske is considered to be a reference point for thinking about information. He was interested in how information could reduce information noise and provide clarity (Dretske, 1981). All information transmission is open to alternatives. As just shown, big data is very much about capturing the noise and alternatives as well, which raw data also contains. One person's noise can be another person's information. In this sense, Dretske's discussion of information does not seem to help us here.

Another discussion of the distinction between data, information and knowledge can be found in the work of Luciano Floridi on the philosophy of information. Floridi (2002) uses an erotetic model to define information, knowledge and data. Erotetic logic is the logic of questions and answers. Then, a piece of data is anything that 'makes a difference', an answer without a question (Floridi, 2002: 106). In terms of big data terminology, it would be something that can be reused and as such makes a difference. In Chapter 6, we shall discuss the use of Apache technologies to extract entities, such as the location of an item or the name of its author. In this way, data or new entities that make a difference are produced from content. At the moment of extraction, we do not know the questions these items might answer.

Information, on the other hand, has a relevant query attached to it, according to Floridi. In Chapter 2, we saw how Tesco collects information from its customers using its Tesco Clubcard system in order to reorganise its own sales processes. Data is collected with the idea of providing answers about customer needs and interests. Floridi (2002) explains that this relevant query does not necessarily need to be answered by an actual piece of data. Misinformation, for instance, is also information, while the existence of God is a relevant question that can only be answered with belief.

What is knowledge, finally? This is one of the oldest questions in philosophy and cannot be answered just in the context of information science. For Floridi (2002), knowledge adds an explanation to information. To get through most activities of our lives, we do not need this; for instance, we can operate a car easily without knowing how it works exactly, or why it works in that way. Our worldview is determined by information or relevant questions we ask of data. In information science, too, there remains a lingering doubt about the need to develop knowledge engineering, and whether information might not be enough for our daily digital interactions (Wilson, 2002).

What is the place of content assets or even digital media in this distinction of data, information and knowledge? Content certainly spans information and data, and for some authors such as David Nuescheler, who is behind various content repository specifications (Gottlieb, 2008), 'everything is content'. However, for others, content is not data (Gottlieb, 2008), as it is (a) trying to communicate something and (b) is often intended for a human audience. Content is different from data. For instance, content is necessary, as 'people don't do data well. Automated systems do... We ought to remember a lot more from William Kent, about the ambiguities of concepts, but especially that bit about computers possessing incredibly little ordinary intelligence' (Ashley, 2013).

Big data, however, repurposes content for machine consumption, and is about taking back content to its most fundamental items that make a difference, thus allowing meaning to emerge and therefore be reused, first by machines, but, in the end, also by humans. In *Big Data – A Revolution that will Transform How we Live Work and Think*, Mayer-Schönberger and Cukier give another definition of data and link it to the idea of a 'given' or a 'fact' (Mayer-Schönberger and Cukier, 2013: 78). Data is everything that can be digitally repurposed and analysed by machines in the first instance. Not everything digital can be data, as we have discussed throughout this book, and raw content is a prime suspect for being outside the data life cycle.

In the words of Mayer-Schönberger and Cukier, content needs to be 'datafied' in order to be repurposed. 'To datafy a phenomenon is to put it in a quantified format so that it can be tabulated and analysed', they argue (Mayer-Schönberger and Cukier, 2013: 78). This is different from the process of producing a digital surrogate based on digitising originally analogue content, and indeed one of the biggest confusions of big data is simply to count the number of bits and bytes that come out of these digitisation processes. Mayer-Schönberger and Cukier (2013) rightly point out that big data is related not so much to the tradition of digitisation, but to the desire to produce quantifiable pieces of information or data a computer can ask relevant questions against. Big data is therefore 'big' in terms of the number of items in it that make a difference, and not simply in terms of bits and bytes.

As we have already seen in Chapter 2, there seems to be much confusion in the definition of big data. Possibly the most famous definition of big data, given by Doug Laney in 2001, only describes various features, the three Vs: 'Big data is high volume, high velocity, and/or high variety information assets that require new forms of processing to enable enhanced decision making, insight discovery and process optimization' (quoted in Beyer and Laney, 2012). High volume, or the first V, means that big data needs a certain size to be big. As seen in Chapter 2, this volume is often linked to data that is produced not just once, but again and again, as a result of an experiment or as an ongoing conversation on Twitter, for example. Any statically produced data will at some point be not big enough any more to count as big. Therefore, the second V, or velocity, is important. The third V relates to something we have not really analysed in detail yet. Variety of big data assets in terms of formats, origins, etc. is an important feature of any kind of big data processing. It is often the combination of various information asset repositories that enables the productive exploitation of big data. We shall see later in this chapter how new technologies had to emerge to allow for the collection of these items.

The three Vs provide a description rather than a definition. However, they allow us to incorporate as many perspectives as possible in big data. Defining big data will always be difficult, as we cannot give an absolute definition of 'big'. Something is never big enough to count as big data, as there is no measure that would give a clear answer, because 'data can be big in different ways' (Lynch, 2008). To illustrate his claim, Clifford Lynch compares commonly quoted examples of large data sets from CERN and telescopes with data that is big due to its lasting significance and that needs to be kept for future reuse. For Lynch (2008), big data is a data stewardship task, where data needs to be described appropriately with metadata so that it can be reused in the future work.

While Lynch's focus on preservation and long-term availability of big data is different from ours, which concentrates on use, we nevertheless agree with him that what really matters in big data is its (long-term) often unforeseen use. Only through its use does big data become big, as it often consists of the combination of many smaller data sets that are used together to drive analytics. The use also determines what we are interested in and why we attempt big data in the first place. As seen in Chapter 4, open data is in this sense closely linked to big data and, while open data is not a condition for big data, it certainly makes big data much easier, which is one reason why scientists are so interested in open data. Open data enables the new analytics that are pursued in science (Dobo and Steed, 2012).

In many other computing areas, it is use or function that defines an object. In 'duck typing', for instance, methods and functions determine the valid object's semantics. The duck test by James Whitcomb Riley is applied: 'When I see a bird that walks like a duck and swims like a duck and quacks like a duck, I call that bird a duck' (Wikipedia, 2013a). In this sense, data is big data when it walks and quacks like big data, when it behaves like big data and is used as such. This is how we shall see it. Big data is big to us if a certain use is implied, which we analyse in this section, and if this use challenges the underlying ecosystems of crowds and clouds. Then, even relatively small data sets can be big data because of the way they are used in computational analytics.

As we have already concluded in Chapter 2, in order to make new use happen with big data, a digital ecosystem is needed. The new large amounts of data we have to deal with drive the rethinking of networks and division of work that lies at the heart of the digital ecosystem evolution. It was not by chance that digital ecosystems started their development with the emergence of big data. As discussed in Chapter 2, digital ecosystems have been developed to enable data as a platform (Lohman, 2013). All the technologies and methodologies of digital ecosystems that we have analysed are developments that help realise big data as a platform. Crowds and clouds support the datafication that underlies big data as well as the analytics.

Saleh et al. (2013) analyse in more detail how big data thrives through digital ecosystems by providing various examples. In big data digital ecosystems, the providers of platforms or cloud operators will collaborate with those who collect the data. Together, they will function as bridges linking diverse organisations. For the purposes of our analysis, big data organisations will be all those that are involved in the use of big data. They might have a lot of data themselves, they might possess analytical capacities, or they might be just involved as parts of the digital ecosystem that helps big data to create value. Saleh et al. (2013) report some unusual examples for such big data organisations if, for example, consumer crowds of car industry products collaborate with insurance owners. The boundaries between organisations, which had been more strongly separated until recently, will be blurred if sensors in cars offer direct input to car insurance companies on the driving behaviour of their insured drivers. This in turn will have potentially difficult implications for the legal and ethical frameworks under which these organisations operate, and will call into action governments and other regulators. In this way, the ecosystem expands around the data and its use.

Saleh et al. (2013) present a new type of big data organisation that will participate in the data platforms of the future. These might be those organisations that also have other cloud products or completely separate ones, but in any case these will be an essential component in the exploitation of big data. All these organisations need to show that they can cooperate. Borgman et al. (2012) discuss the example of cooperation around data in distributed science organisations with the aim to develop joint development scenarios. They conclude that data have become 'boundary objects, both bridging and demarcating the lines between communities' (Borgman et al., 2012: 488). 'Boundary object' refers here to the work of Susan Leigh Star:

> Boundary objects are objects, which are both plastic enough to adapt to local needs and constraints of the several parties employing them, yet robust enough to maintain a common identity across sites... The creation and management of boundary objects is key in developing and maintaining coherence across intersecting social worlds.
>
> (Star, 1992: 406)

Boundary objects therefore ensure that meaning is transported between organisations. Accordingly, Bruno Latour refers to 'immutable mobiles' (Latour, 1990) for those objects that transport meaning between organisations.

Data has become a boundary object in organisations for a while. Redman (2008) has demonstrated how following the flow of data in an organisation can be an excellent means to understanding its deeper workings. Yet only since big data has pushed the 'datafication of everything' (Mayer-Schönberger and Cukier, 2013) in an organisation have these boundary objects really determined the final components of any business and also of private life. Personal exercise, for instance, is today datafied if our gym activities are guided by a detailed analysis of the impact of running, weightlifting, etc. on heart rates, fat–muscle ratio and so on. We can also track our children's movements using the GPS in their smartphones if we want to. The digital asset management enterprise is no exception to this datafication of everything. We have already seen here how content becomes datafied using technologies like information extraction, or by employing customer feedback on media so that the content can then be reused later. For Mohanty et al. (2013), digital asset management is at the very heart of the evolution of big data organisations.

Lycett (2013) gives us a good example of how datafication progresses in the digital media and asset industries, using Netflix. This organisation works permanently on its own content datafication using crowds and clouds. Lycett (2013) describes how Netflix's video assets became dematerialised in the shift from a traditional mail-order video rental towards a fully digital streaming service. The streaming model also means that much more data can be collected than could have been present in a traditional catalogue. Netflix now knows how much time its crowds spend on watching a particular film, when they watch, what else they will watch on the same occasion, which films are watched together and so on. In short, it has a range of data items that make a difference to the business model at its disposal. The amount of data on the relationship between customer, film and Netflix is further improved by the interactions that can take place with the crowds that gather around the films and other content. Social influence can be used to improve the sales of films. But this is only the beginning. Netflix has also begun to produce its own film assets, where production decisions are directly influenced by the data it gathers from past consumer behaviour (Lycett, 2013). It has thus demonstrated that the datafication of assets implies the integration of crowds on a platform that links the data gained from the crowds with these assets.

A brief history of big data

The development of big data technologies and organisations has not started in business. Science has taken a lead. Thus one of the best ways to take a historical view of big data is to look at the history of CERN, the European Organization for Nuclear Research. CERN is the original big data organisation.

The best history of big data can be watched at *http://whatsthebigdata.com/2013/09/04/the-evolution-of-big-data-at-cern-and-everywhere-else-animation*. It is better than others, as it draws on the history of big data in the science communities and especially in particle physics. The film explains that for decades, CERN has been struggling with the amount of data its experiments produced. In a sense, CERN can claim to be the world's first big data organisation. Yet, not only the amount of data was a problem. Researchers also had to travel to CERN to access the data and connect to other networks, too, in order to retrieve all the data in context. In 1970, CERNET was developed, before a newly established Internet remote access connection was established at the end of the 1980s. In order to allow further sharing of research results, the World Wide Web protocol was added in the 1990s and, as seen in Chapter 3, helped people to exchange research documents and articles.

Over time, the CERN data kept growing and in the 2000s its network capacities could again not keep up with the need of its users. A complete redesign of its networking capacities had become necessary. It became physically impossible to store and analyse all the CERN data in one location. The data needed to be distributed. CERN researchers began to share not just the research articles via the Internet, but also the resources necessary to create this research, including the data. The GRID computing network (Foster et al., 2008) was born and with it the final stage in the evolution of computer networks towards big data clouds.

The GRID followed the utopian ideal of sharing resources in a free association of scientists. It was, in this sense, a continuation of the promises of the republic of letters (Daston, 1991) and its ideal of scholarly collaboration and communication from the eighteenth century. It used journal articles to exchange information and included everyone who was part of the scholarly process – not just professors, but private scholars, librarians, archivists, etc. For the GRID communities, it was not the ideal that changed, but the means of communication. The idea of the GRID amended the article towards sharing of resources. If the first evolution of the web shared documents and the second shared data, as discussed in Chapter 3, the third would share resources. Most importantly, the GRID was about sharing not just computing and data resources but also user innovation (Blanke et al., 2009). This focus was on agency with data and computing.

The promise of the GRID has, however, not materialised. The GRID has not become the commercial success its inventors had anticipated, as it required a level of willingness to share and trust that cannot be taken for granted outside a close-knit community such as that of particle physicists, for instance. The cloud is a more business-oriented approach towards accessing remote resources that does not require subscribing to the utopian ideals of sharing upon which the GRID was based. While science was the original driver behind big data, the latter has become very popular recently, given that other societal actors such as business and government have taken it up. Virtually every part of society now collects data or little digital things that make a difference to them. These actors need cloud models, not GRID ones.

The GRID was the first type of cloud that helped the particle physics community work together. Its sharing model is very close to the ecosystem ideals of self-organisation, scalability and sustainability, and it linked scientific crowds to shared resources. Following the GRID, crowd applications in many domains continue to be successful at creating larger and larger computing resources that could deal with a wide range of data challenges. In Chapter 3, we discussed mainly crowd applications that complemented computer reasoning in order to take on tasks that computers are not so good at. Next to these, there has always been another strong tradition in crowd-computing that is occupied with linking not human resources but computing resources across the Internet. Humans only play a role here in as much as they are the providers of underused computing resources.

We have already encountered the best-known project of this kind in Chapter 3, when we discussed the BOINC crowd infrastructure. BOINC (Berkeley Open Infrastructure for Network Computing) was developed out of the SETI@home work, or as the result of this experiment in public-resource computing by D. P. Anderson et al. (2002). It is associated with the SETI (Search for Extra-terrestrial Intelligence) project to detect signals in space that could indicate intelligent life outside earth. SETI@home employs underused desktop computers on the Internet to decode radio signals from space.

For the scientists, this was a revolution in the involvement of the public and pre-dated the success of the Galaxy Zoo collective intelligence by a couple of years. Some scientists even thought if the 'screen savers of the world had united', they would have dwarfed any existing supercomputer (Shirts and Pande, 2006). The reference to screen savers indicates how these projects harvest computing cycles from crowds. As soon as the screen saver appears on a local desktop, it will activate a tool that the crowd participant had downloaded before. This tool connects to a central data repository to download scientific data that is processed while the local desktop remains idle. The results are merged back into the data sets on the server and can be analysed by the scientists.

Next to SETI@home, the most successful project of this kind was *www.climateprediction.net*, a collaboration between the BBC, several UK universities and the UK Met Office. Climateprediction.net helps improve climate models by going through a wide range of parameters, varying these and rejecting those that fail to predict past climate behaviour. This is not possible with current supercomputers, but it is a task that is perfectly suited for distribution across many remote resources. Climateprediction.net has quickly become the largest climate change experiment and has created one of the biggest computers the world has ever experienced, as measured in the number of cycles it has run. It is therefore a perfect example of how computational collective intelligence can develop. The crowds do not actively contribute their intelligence, but their resources. The big climate data is cut into smaller pieces and distributed for analysis.

With their model of passive participation, these crowd-computing projects have at the same time prepared the evolution of the GRID into the cloud to analyse big data. It is one side of the 'human experience of big data' (Grinter, 2013), which is yet to be fully explored by research. As part of this experience, the crowds do not intervene and offer their computational resources. The cloud effaces the ideals of scientific sharing that the GRID relied on and makes it commercially viable. Where GRIDs enabled access to shared computing resources, clouds provide for 'leased' computing resources on a pay-per-use basis, as seen in Chapter 3. Clouds are generally owned by larger corporations (Foster et al., 2008). Overall, they are more reliable and often easier to use than the complicated GRID networks.

Clouds have turned out to be better instruments for big data than GRIDs, as they emphasise content and data collection rather than data and content sharing. They enable the most important activity in the big data era, the amassing of ever-larger amounts of data and content. Data clouds have been designed with data and content collecting in mind. In the big data era, those who have the data hold the strings (Mayer-Schönberger and Cukier, 2013). Marissa Mayer, Google's former VP of Search Products and User Experience, confessed some years ago (Perez, 2007) that possessing data is nowadays often more important than having the right algorithmic reasoning. Here, we would like to expand on this idea of collecting items that make a difference as the main activity in the big data age, and focus on the new emerging crowds and clouds techniques that enable this transformation.

Mayer-Schönberger and Cukier (2013) argue that the ability to programme big data and extract value is initially the most important factor in the big data era. Gradually, however, these abilities will become more commonplace. Then, it will be the data itself that will be the most costly part in big data business. New 'data intermediaries' (Mayer-Schönberger and Cukier, 2013: 135) are already emerging that collect data from a variety of sources and prepare it for reuse. They exploit the fact that data has become 'an asset independent of what it had previously aimed to measure' (ibid.: 136). This is the reason companies have welcomed the cloud – it gives them the chance to hold on to their own data and share it in doses that suits their needs. Sharing can be done with clouds as needed, while with GRIDs it had to be done, as it was part of their design.

The data cloud technologies that have been developed to support this new value from big data allow collecting the data as it is. Thus, intermediaries can concentrate on their biggest challenge, which will be to build up the trust necessary to collect the data in the first place. A big obstacle in this trust would be the downward demand to transform the data in order to make it fit the intermediaries' data stores. It is part of the business model of these intermediaries that data is always good enough and does not need to be perfect to be accepted by them. In fact, the messier the data, the stronger the claim by the intermediaries that only they can make it worthwhile.

The intermediaries therefore need to rely on infrastructures that allow them to process the data as they find it. The new NoSQL technologies, introduced in Chapter 3, are able to do that. While the name goes back to the late 1990s, it was Eric Evans from Rackspace who made the term popular at an event on open-source distributed databases (Wikipedia, 2013c). NoSQL technologies stand for the realisation that most of the world's usable information does not come along in (database) tables. Collectors will not be interested in the shape that their objects of desire take and the materials they are made of. All they want to do is collect things that make a difference – perhaps not now, but potentially in the future. Collectors want data for some potential future usage they might not even know about right now. NoSQL technologies are made to capture all the data as it appears. Without them, the datafication of everything would be limited to what counts as data in databases.

Dobo and Steed (2012) discuss research on how NoSQL technologies can support the datafication of digital media assets. In their example application, 3D media assets for visualisations are edited by many authors using a range of modelling tools. The challenge is to synchronise the sharing of the 3D models based on strict revision control. Instead of traditional file-based systems, Dobo and Steed (2012) experimented with NoSQL databases, which have proven to be more flexible and allow the storage of 3D scenes separately, without giving up on revision control.

Traditional databases were made for tables, and not for such 3D multimedia assets. They were designed with ACID in mind. ACID stands for four key properties all traditional databases had: atomicity, consistency, isolation and durability.

- Atomicity implies that any transaction running against the database is executed as a whole or aborted.
- Consistency is the assurance that the whole database is always in a consistent state.
- Isolation means that transactions run separately from each other.
- Durability safeguards against loss of data due to power failures, etc.

While these ACID features are important properties for data in traditional applications such as financial reporting, implementing a system for collecting real-life data that stems from a range of sources and that is at the same time fully ACID-compliant is often difficult. NoSQL technologies offer some compromises, which make this work easier (F. Chang et al., 2008). In Chapter 3, we discussed their use in the ecosystem world as a new web architecture technology, while here we concentrate on the data and query model. These are the two most important features that allow for large-scale collecting of items that make a difference. Other commonly discussed features, such as sharding, mainly relate to the way in which the data is distributed.

One of the simplest versions of NoSQL are key-value stores. They operate like a phone book, where we can use the name of a person to look up an associated telephone number. The name is the key and phone number the value. Key-value stores include Amazon's Dynamo store (DeCandia et al., 2007), which realises a simple key-value store, where anything can be a key to a stored digital objects. The query model of this NoSQL store is therefore to retrieve data based on a uniquely assigned key. Key-value stores allow for any kind of data model to be used to store the data. They are very useful to store and quickly access large amounts of data, but are less useful if particular data items are sought, for which the key is not known.

The famous Amazon data cloud S3 operates under this model. Here, the collections of items are called buckets and are thought of as containers for data. All data is dropped in these buckets and retrieved from them. Scaling out is straightforward, as the buckets can be distributed easily across different computer resources. Key-value stores should be avoided, however, if one is interested in developing fast access to individual data items for single applications (Redmond et al., 2012), because they are made for mass-collecting.

Next to key-value stores such as Amazon's S3, document databases dominate the NoSQL landscape. They store documents, often encoded in various XML formats and with fast access to them through keys that can also index the parts of the XML documents. Documents are seen as the most basic unit of data. For instance, document databases such as CouchDB allow only for an update of the whole document. To perform an update to only parts of it, the whole document first needs to be retrieved, then changed and finally stored again as a whole. As the web is made up of documents, these document stores are also seen as 'made for the web'. They have their limitations, however, because anything smaller than a document, but still an item that makes a difference, is difficult to retrieve and store in document databases.

Both document databases and key-value stores are been designed for producing and querying the big analytics using the new big data computing paradigm of MapReduce. This allows collectors to access quickly the whole of their collections and reduce these to desirable outputs. MapReduce is Google's answer to the big data challenge in order to process large amounts of data in distributed data sets (Dean and Ghemawat, 2008). It is made for 'raw data' that is messy and can perform calculations on the whole of this raw data. Google simply abstracted what most of the data operations entailed, as their senior engineers have argued:

> We realized that most of our computations involved applying a map operation to each logical record in our input in order to compute a set of intermediate key/value pairs, and then applying a reduce operation to all the values that shared the same key, in order to combine the derived data appropriately.
>
> (Dean and Ghemawat, 2008)

MapReduce is best explained with the same phone book illustration from above. Let's say we would like to count the number of people in the phone book having Adam as their first name. As phone books are generally sorted according to last name, we need to go through the whole phone book. In the map step, we would simply traverse the whole phone book and, each time we find an Adam, replace the phone number with a '1'. The reduce step would then reduce all these 1s by adding them up to give the total number of Adams in the phone book.

MapReduce is one of the most powerful frameworks for bundling data and then applying global analysis on this data. It is based on Google's recognition that its raw data from the web or sometimes even raw content such as documents does not fit into the tables of normal databases (Whitehorn, 2013). MapReduce is made for its global operations to index, for instance, the whole web corpus. Mayer-Schönberger and Cukier speak of an 'N=all' analysis (Mayer-Schönberger and Cukier, 2013: 47) in order to indicate that it is not samples that are sought from the data sets any more, but the complete data set is analysed.

MapReduce frameworks are intended for global analysis in big data. The map step in MapReduce can, however, also be seen as a filter to ease the N=all challenge. In the example above, we took out all the non-relevant information, i.e. everyone not called Adam. As part of the desire to cover as much data as possible in big data, it is sometimes forgotten that big data is as much about 'slicing and dicing' the data into the right proportions that allow for the further analytics to happen. We want to have all the 'data in the wild', but we also want to look at it from different angles. Each angle will point out some items of information that are more interesting than others. In this way, bias in the data set is avoided and new models can flourish.

CERN has followed the slice-and-dice model for a while by forming the GRID that distributed the data across the world of physics. Physicists who receive the data are often only interested in smaller chunks and throw the rest away. Once the model of CERN is understood, it is also clear that for successful big data analysis, results will come not just from the large-scale analysis of complete and aggregated data sets, but also come from slicing and dicing the sets into those that are useful. Pollock (2013) contends that the real practices of big data lie in 'decentralized data wrangling' using 'small pieces', which are analytically joined.

Opportunities from big data analysis will not just come from N=all, but from N=all/M. It will come from 'small data', which is another concept that has recently gained prominence. It emphasises the fact that 'insights can be found at any level' (Boyd and Crawford, 2012). Small data is then a reflection of the real practices of big data beyond 'Hey, there's more data than we can process!' (Pollock, 2013), which, as Jacobs (2009) analyses, is one of the biggest misperceptions of big data leading to its pathologies. MapReduce works for big and small data. First, data needs to be sliced into separate buckets or collections one can manage by oneself and then 'reduce' the results of these separate analyses into the overall summative assessment of big data.

MapReduce is part of Google's statements of faith for big data. Among these, the most famous comes from Google's Director of Research Peter Norvig and colleagues, who have defined the 'Unreasonable Effectiveness of Data': 'Simple models and a lot of data trump more elaborate models based on less data.' Their recommendation is to 'follow the data' (Halevy et al., 2009) and build your analysis strategies around the data. NoSQL and MapReduce allow for exactly this. Amatriain (2012) presents how this 'effectiveness of data' quote is often misrepresented as arguing for data and against theory and method. Badly designed theories are also not helped with more evidence from data. Using an example from the world of digital media, Pilászy and Tikk (2009) argue that with regard to the Netflix prize data, ratings from users trump more content information about the films from sources such as IMDb.

So, more data does not necessarily trump better data. We still have to understand what kind of data we need. MapReduce also helps us achieve this by reducing the data to what we need from the N=all situation, where all the data is the sample (N) and comes in varying shapes and forms. At the same time, we want the N=all situation to remain available to us. Here lies the hidden information and the data relevant to queries that have not been asked yet. Using NoSQL technologies, we could make use much more of the data in content, which we could not otherwise fit into traditional databases.

Given that so many items that can make a difference were hidden before, for Marshall, 'Big Data is surely the Gold Rush of the Information Age' (Marshall, 2012: 213). She refers to the enthusiasm in social sciences research about mining Twitter and to the Digital Humanities studies on the Google Books corpus. The Google Ngram viewer (*http://books.google.com/ngrams*) allows users to track the use of words over time from the millions of books Google has digitised. For the first time, the Ngram viewer enables the public to access the millions of words in books and run their own linguistic analysis. Marshall (2012) quotes researchers as the primary parties interested in big data. In the next section, we expand her discussion, which has focused on research, by introducing applications from social media applications as well as government and business to examine the big data gold rush, following our general focus in this book.

Applications in the big data 'gold rush'

Social media is, in many ways, the perfect domain for big data. It delivers velocity, as there are millions of tweets produced every day. As there are also so many citizens of the social media space, the volume of tweets produced is very high, too. In the introduction, we have already discussed how in fact much of big data is identified with social media as such, as this is where most people directly experience it. Yet, as social media is mainly human-created data, it comes in many different versions and types. *The New Scientist*, for instance, reports on the large number of new words that Twitter has inspired (Giles, 2012).

The numbers are simply staggering even in the world of the digital. According to Baek et al. (2011), 70 billion pieces of content are shared daily on Facebook. There are 200 million daily tweets, without mentioning the smartphone social activities that today exceed traditional computer environments by far. This data is held by surprisingly few organisations – mainly social media giants like Google and Facebook, but also a few data intermediaries. The value of this big social data often does not lie in its primary use value, but in what else can be done with it. Companies discovered this a long time ago and offer 'free services' to us like email or online storage in order to access new data. As John Naughton noted in the *Guardian*, we 'pay' for all those free online services these companies offer in a 'different currency, namely your personal data' (Naughton, 2013). Here, it is not primary usage that interests the big data companies, but the secondary usage. Therefore, companies 'work the crowd' (Brown, 2012) to enable this secondary usage.

For Marshall (2012) and Mayer-Schönberger and Cukier (2013), the Google Ngram viewer referenced above is a perfect example of how content such as texts can be 'datafied' by splitting it up into Ngrams or smaller chunks of data. Ngrams are here simply 'n' letters in a word joined together. The word data, for instance, contains two 3-grams: 'dat' and 'ata'. Ngrams are often used in linguistic analysis to counteract the challenges of heterogeneous data, if, for instance, OCRed texts contain recognition errors. Ngrams help with processing those words with inaccuracies. The content-to-data pipeline is key to exploiting big social data.

Twitter in particular, as a kind of real-time record of human digital life, has seen a wide range of secondary usage of its datafied tweets. The current 'gold rush' with Twitter lies in almost real-time sentiment analysis and opinion mining (Pang and Lee, 2008) to read the state of mind of organisations, consumers, politicians and other opinion-makers. Twitter now appears to be the 'echo chamber of people's opinions' (Van Dijck and Poell, 2013: 9). Companies, policy researchers and many others have always depended on being able to track what people believe and think. Twitter and its fellow citizens in the social data space have given them completely new means to do this. Twitter prepares its content as data that could feed sentiment analysis techniques.

Pang and Lee (2008) quote statistics that let any digital marketing person hold their breath. For example, 81 per cent of Internet users try to find out information about products online, with almost a fifth of users doing this daily. What is perhaps even more relevant to our investigation is that consumers are willing to pay a significant premium for five-star-rated items rather than four-star, with a third of online consumers having provided a review themselves. These statistics were captured even before Twitter had its breakthrough and gave access to opinions for marketers, in real-time as well as in historical relation, by providing a time axis that allows the tracking of opinions on a subject over the history of tweets about it. These tweets now include not only textual content but also images and videos, especially through Twitter's new Vine platform (Rohrer, 2013). Rohrer also mentions problems with keeping track of the Vine video content, as it is more difficult to datafy and therefore filter with automated means. For instance, a porn film was picked as an editor's choice.

Images and videos still feature very little in sentiment analysis, because this type of analysis relies largely on the word or the Ngram as its basic unit to understand people's opinions. Here, the phrase 'great offer' next to a product name will make the company happier than a comment claiming the product to be a waste of money. In order to understand such differences, sentiment analysis systems employ dictionaries (such as SentiWordNet) to a large extent, combined with prior knowledge of what kind of phrases express a positive or negative sentiment. Otherwise, sentiment analysis trusts other traditional machine learning and text analysis techniques, but applied to subjective statements and with the aim to capture the subjective content of these statements.

Sentiment analysis pushes traditional text analysis techniques to their limit. These, for instance, often struggle to capture negations. However, learning about the polarity of expression is of key importance to understanding opinions. The expression 'I like cola' differs strongly from its negation 'I do not like cola'. Wiegand et al. (2010) provide a survey of existing negation-tracking techniques for sentiment analysis. For machines, the language of opinions and sentiments is complicated, as a 'not' can also express a positive attitude: 'Cola not only tastes great, it is also cheap.' Things get even more complicated, as there is irony and the different use of negation in various language, etc. All this makes sentiment analysis a complex computational task.

Mayer-Schönberger and Cukier (2013) report little on the problems with sentiment analysis, but rather on its spectacular successes such as the prediction of the box-office performance of Hollywood films based on the number of tweets about a particular film. Tweets can also signal the performance of stocks, offering insights on the emotional state of those involved with companies in order to understand their fortunes. These successful examples of Twitter as an echo chamber are, however, often based on very distinct linguistic domains that come with highly concentrated areas such as stock market brokers. In the wider world, most people talk about brands neither in a positive nor negative way, but just express mere 'statements of facts and information' (Rhodes,

2010). Most online discussions are neutral and cannot be used to track sentiments and opinions.

The data extracted from these conversations is not neutral either. The social media platforms or clouds also shape the data that describes the crowds. Gitelman's (2013) critique that 'raw data is an oxymoron' is aptly made. 'Raw data is both an oxymoron and a bad idea; to the contrary, data should be cooked with care' (Bowker, 2005: 183; see also Boyd and Crawford, 2012). However, this might not be what is so exciting about mining Twitter for opinions. Rather, it is more the real-time analytics abilities that generate the interest in its datafication of opinions, according to Van Dijck and Poell (2013), who cite the ability of public health officials to track epidemics in real time by analysing tweets about users' state of health and potential symptoms. At the same time, public health information can be fed back into Twitter to help fight and contain the disease by publishing information fast and in near real-time to users.

Opinion mining is just one example of how social media applications have transformed Twitter, Facebook and others into 'big data firms' (Van Dijck and Poell, 2013: 8), with a business model built around data that can be repurposed. Governments, too, have become big data firms and make use of Twitter to monitor their own populations (Van Dijck and Poell, 2013). For instance, the police can use Twitter to coordinate their response to riots and civil unrest. Procter et al. (2013a) discuss the example of the 2011 London riots. While Twitter had been used by rioters to coordinate their actions, the police were against shutting down the service completely during the riots, as it helped them with their own responses. However, as shown in follow-up research by Procter et al. (2013b), there are still considerable problems for policing to make effective use of social media, mainly because the technologies and methodologies have not yet filtered down to the police departments. The police are not alone in this challenge and decisive strategies to use Twitter in computational social analysis are still to be developed. There are problems of scalability if the current, relatively small, test Twitter corpora are to include many more real-time tweets as well as issues with the specific language used in Twitter (Procter et al., 2013b).

Alongside citizens and the police, governments as a whole are using big data and pushing content into it. As discussed in Chapter 4, governments were among the first to open up their data sets and offered to unleash a tsunami of data onto their populations (Rogers, 2010). Harris (2013) reports on ideas held by government officials that big data can create efficiency in various government sectors. For instance, in health care, electronic patient records appear to help evaluate treatments, welfare programmes can be assessed on whether they deliver on their promises, and defence spending could be better controlled. With all of these, it is often the inability of governments to handle integrated data sets that stops them from becoming involved in the big data use. All these are examples of how government departments can be reorganised around 'data that relates to people', where data would not just be the 'exhaust' of providing services, 'but rather become a central asset in trying to figure out how you would improve every aspect of health care' (Economist, 2010).

Governments have had the advantage that they can compel populations to deliver data to them and be datafied; nonetheless, governments have also shown to be ineffective in using the data (Mayer-Schönberger and Cukier, 2013: 116). The open government data story is, as previously seen, also one of giving away data to (commercial) organisations that are better set up to exploit it. More recently, governments, just like big data firms, have started to change their way of working and adjusted their applications around the data that they gather. According to a BBC report by Cellan-Jones (2013), the UK government's digital work has recently undergone a transformation in the aims and objectives. The UK digital government planners realised that the previous attempts to centralise government digitally in one big data integration application have failed. While e-government had previously attempted to set up large-scale projects that aimed to work in five years' time (by which time it would have probably been an outdated service with old data), the digital UK government team now focuses on producing something fast, even though it might fail. Failure is seen as part of a future solution and the process of building it.

The adaptive strategies of the government big data firm have taken a while to be set in place. After all, the government sector has a long history of big data that, in many ways, even pre-dates that of science and dwarfs any commercial effort to collect data. Official national archives and other national memory institutions should become more and more important in a data-driven economy and society, particularly if the holders of data will be the ones who benefit most. Archives should therefore welcome the current push towards big data, but there is still too much uncertainty about their exact role and how they can become a big data player (Blanke and Kristel, 2013).

To this end, the example of a research project to integrate Holocaust research archives is significant (Blanke and Kristel, 2013). The figures can easily be compared with any other big data initiative. Holocaust archives are one of the most commonly used examples for big data in archives. Here, in particular, the 200 TB of the oral history collection of Holocaust survivors funded by the Spielberg foundation are contrasted with 120 TB of the Sloan Digital Sky Survey (as of 2011) by Nature and others (Hand, 2011). According to research by Blanke and Kristel (2013), Holocaust archives hold over 700 TB of digitised material; among these over 600 GB constitute structured information on Holocaust victims. Governments in the Task Force for International Cooperation on Holocaust Education, Remembrance and Research (ITF) have agreed to encourage more open access to Holocaust data in archives (Blanke and Kristel, 2013), which will result in a rapid growth in such materials in the near future.

Government might have plenty of big data, but it is business that currently has the main expertise in exploiting it. One of its leading voices, the *Economist* (2010), announced that there is 'data, data everywhere', with most of it even shared across the Internet. The first example the *Economist* quotes for a data company is Walmart, which we might not normally associate with computing innovations. Walmart has built an Internet of Things into its stores that help it capture one million customer transactions every hour, which has led to big data stores containing several petabytes of data. The website bigdata-startups.com (2013) describes tools and services that have made 'big data part of the DNA of Walmart'. There is, for instance, the Social Genome tool that allows Walmart to send product information to its social media users who mentioned a particular product. Social Genome is a big data mashup of publicly available data and data that Walmart has gathered in its stores. It even pushed Walmart beyond typical MapReduce frameworks so that it had to develop its own high-performance data analysis environment.

Next in the big data product line of Walmart is Shoppycat, which uses Facebook data to recommend Walmart products to Facebook users based on an analysis of their social graph. It also helps find a store that has a particular product a consumer wants on its shelves. Finally, Walmart has developed several smartphone applications, which are supposed to enhance the in-store experience of Walmart customers and connect them to items in its store. In order to make recommendations to online social media users and to track their behaviour, hundreds of millions of key words are analysed daily in the Walmart 'online marketing ecosystem', according to the analysis on bigdata-startups.com (2013).

Walmart is an example for marketing analytics using all available data to build better and better models. N=all implies better digital marketing models using a sophisticated computational ecosystem of crowds and clouds, where Walmart is an example of how shopping crowds are worked on by means of a sophisticated cloud. Big data can also target the small margins. Amazon is one of these big data with small margins companies. Its CEO, Jeff Bezos, said: 'High margins cover a lot of sins. We wouldn't know how to do a high margin business. Low margins keep you aligned with customers' (quoted in Dignan, 2012). The aim is to achieve 'scale without mass' (Brynjolfsson et al., 2008). But only companies that are able to 'diffuse IT' across their operations are able to benefit. For companies like Amazon and Google, this is definitely not a problem.

As retail is generally a low-margin business, Amazon has a long history of partnerships that allow it to distribute its opportunities as widely as possible. Since 1997, Amazon has worked together with AOL (MyCustomer, 2000) and in 2000, Amazon.com services became directly available to AOL users. This made AOL the largest online marketing partner for Amazon. Amazon was interested in harvesting all the user data that AOL produced in those days (Mayer-Schönberger and Cukier, 2013). This helped Amazon develop its famous recommender systems or 'customer-centric analytics' (Wiegand et al., 2010), which in turn laid the foundation for its commercial success. While AOL bet that content and a closed ecosystem would allow it to exploit the Internet's commercial future, Amazon understood earlier that it is the network value of the web that really counts, a topic we shall discuss in detail in the next chapter. One is a rich online participant by what can be done with one's data.

The indubitable 'master' of secondary data exploitation is, however, Google. The search company always has the secondary user in mind (Mayer-Schönberger and Cukier, 2013: 132). Google has continuously strived to expand its access to the user crowd information and wrap it into its platforms in order to improve its marketing and advertising services that have made it so much money (Lohr, 2012). It opened up and just provided freely what was available before only with paid services. From free services such as Gmail and Google Docs, it gets value by exploiting the user data that comes with it. As Crawford and Chau argue, 'integrating all of your digital activities gives Google a more complete picture of your preferences as a user. This in turn enables Google to further differentiate its targeted advertising proposition' (Crawford and Chau, 2013). Therefore, big user data creates a 'dangling value' (ibid.) for Google that allows the search company to monetise its users' culture, feeling, opinions, etc. Google here follows its own knowledge of how to link key words in users' queries with feelings in order to advertise products.

Big data Google makes the small margins count. Google certainly earns a lot of money from advertising mass products, but its services really make a difference for distributing products its customers had never dreamt of purchasing. Because Google objectifies their culture through its keyword systems, it is able to move their desires beyond what they are already interested in. This author, for instance, uses his Gmail account to communicate with fellow researchers and academics around the world. He is therefore blessed with a steady stream of advertisements for overseas degrees that do not require any qualification to begin studying. Maybe, this tells me that I should be really interested in another PhD.

Pushing PhDs onto me is one example of how Google believes its services to be able to predict my presence as its user (Choi and Varian, 2012). The company has even created a prediction API (Pouilloux, 2011) to make this happen, which gives access to Google's cloud-based machine-learning tools. The API is based on the earlier and better documented work on Google trends (Choi and Varian, 2012), which provided a time-series index of user queries entered into Google per geographic location (per country or US state). The trends tools are freely available under *http://google.com/trends*. Choi and Varian (2012) offer various examples of how 'predicting the present' works. There are, for instance, more queries on shipping prices during the major shopping seasons of the year. Other presence predictions include sales of motor vehicles and parts, numbers of newly unemployed and travel destinations.

Google made headlines with its presence analysis tools by demonstrating how they could foretell the H1N1 (swine) flu virus spread. It was observed that search behaviour changed during H1N1, 'particularly in the categories influenza complications and term for influenza' (Cook et al., 2011). Internet search terms can, however, also mean a different presence. Dugas et al. (2012) demonstrate some of the problems of tracking diseases with Google trends. For instance, during the bird flu outbreak in 2010, people started searching for symptoms in regions where there were no registered cases. The search crowd is not always rational in its behaviour.

The predictions of the present exploit the fact that in all these cases online crowds will gather around particular search terms. Google trends simply analyse this relationship between a change in information flow and changes in the present real life. Trends is therefore close to Google's natural habitat of analysing search queries in order to understand Internet users. Search queries give any analyst a very good indicator about information needs of online crowds. *https://developers.google.com/bigquery* is a Google service for companies to plug into these data sets. Google flu analysis might struggle with predicting the presence of flu at times, but it can become a gold mine for any pharmaceutical company for improving online sales or helping it guess how to distribute its products in case of epidemics.

Google is a big data company, as it has the data others need to do their own analytics. We have seen throughout the discussions in this book how Google tries to occupy the space of the 'man in the middle', the intermediary without which others cannot build their own ecosystem. Kelly (2012) asks in his blog, on the contrary, why the company that invented MapReduce appears to be a latecomer in the commercial big data space, where others seemingly dominate the cloud space. This impression reduces big data to cloud technologies, and Google clearly is a big data company. Just because Amazon has the most successful cloud service, this does not make it a commercial big data player. In our example above, it was rather its ability to reuse and combine data in new ways once it joined forces with AOL that made it a big data organisation. Google has the advantage that its data sits at the heart of everything that seems possible in big data analytics right now. Through its searchers, it knows what the crowds are interested in.

Regalado (2013) raises another concern of Google when it comes to big data. When contacted about some interviews with staff, a Google PR person told him that Google does not like the term 'big data': 'It's too Big Brother-ish.' Regalado then started to search Google's press releases and could not find anything on big data. It might appear in Google job ads, but is seemingly avoided by the Google PR machine.

Google is not alone in this idea that big data has too much in common with Big Brother. We have actually known for a long time that the National Security Agency in the USA collects billions of emails and builds one of the largest data centres in the world (Mayer-Schönberger and Cukier, 2013). Yet only since its former contractor Edward Snowden spoke to the press has this knowledge been brought to public attention with more concrete cases and revealed the full reach of the NSA. For Snowden, it is Orwell's *1984* but this time for real, as 'the Internet is a TV that watches you' (Regalado, 2013).

Critiques and limitations of big data

Big data has always been the occupation of those concerned with controlling others: 'After all, [big data] isn't that new. The Romans and the Nazis amassed huge amounts of data on their populations' (Schradie, 2013). The new digital big data goes much further here. It is not just a challenge for technologies, business models, etc., but also for more fundamental questions of how we would like to live together. It is necessary to ask questions about who will benefit most from big data and at what costs. Once we have collected all this data, once collecting has become part of our (digital) lives and surrounds us in digital ecosystems, critical questions emerge about what all this data means, who owns the data and what kind of analysis we want to do with it rather than just what we can do with it. Otherwise, according to Schradie (2013), a new digital divide looms between big data rich and big data poor.

Big data leaves out many things and leaves some of us poor. There are, first of all, those things that cannot be datafied, or can be so only with significant loss. Digital things and content have to be transformed to become data. Lisa Gitelman called this the 'imagination of data' (Gitelman, 2013). Although imagination is possibly too strong a term, Gitelman points out that there are limitations to datafication; this is not only because not everything can be quantified and datafied as seen, for instance, with regard to sentiment mining, but also because some quantifications carry mistakes that are multiplied once combined with other quantifications. A good example of the latter are the problems text analysis algorithms have with OCRed texts. Even minor inaccuracies from the OCR will lead to the wrong extraction of texts, as many of the text analysis tools depend on syntactic analysis at least for the initial analysis of data (K. Jung et al., 2004). It is no surprise, then, that the quantification of human information is not perfect, but this is sometimes forgotten once the magical word 'data' is brought into play.

Even if datafication were perfect, the question remains: what and who does it not cover? These are the big data poor: 'Big data and whole data are also not the same... The current ecosystem around Big Data creates a new kind of digital divide: the Big Data rich and the Big Data poor' (Boyd and Crawford, 2012: 169). Against all predictions, there are still many people outside the clouds. Looking back at Google's flu predictions, it might be that exactly those crowds who are affected most by the flu epidemic are not in Google's ecosystems. 'Who is the most vulnerable for the flu? The poor and elderly. Who is least likely to be online? The poor and the elderly' (Schradie, 2013). Those who are part of the digital production crowds are even fewer. Lerman (2013) compares the hypothetical case of a typical 'big data rich' person with a poor one and claims the right for the latter 'not to be forgotten'. The big data revolution needs to be 'just' and include everyone, otherwise it will be a threat to 'equality'.

In Chapter 4, we introduced the idea of an equality architecture in order to make open data just and avoid its use by the rich and powerful only. An important component of this equality architecture was to let everyone participate equally in the analysis of open data, mainly by including a transformation of the crowds by educating them in the effective use of open data. We offered some examples that also demonstrated how difficult such participation would be. For big data, this kind of wider participation through education seems even more difficult to realise, and we are only at the beginning of an emerging debate on how this might be possible. For instance, M. Smith et al. (2012) present how location awareness in smartphones can be used to create 'privacy zones' in order to exclude undesirable media from reaching smartphones.

Big data algorithms are complex and require a deeper understanding of applied mathematics. They also make it necessary to invest in and understand complex computational ecosystems. How can individuals take data ownership and even use big data for the personal benefits when it requires very large and expensive infrastructures for companies to exploit its benefits? The data sets themselves have become more and more expensive – who will be able to afford them? Manovich captures this problem when he points out that '[w]hile a number of free data analysis and visualisation tools have become available on the web during last few years... they are not useful unless you have access to large social data sets' (Manovich, 2011), which are normally not publicly available.

Even where we seemingly have an abundance of data and a large participation of the crowd, it is still not evident that big data analysis will add to our existing understanding. Boyd and Crawford (2012) and Procter et al. (2013b) discuss how the excitement about the Twitter and Facebook 'social graph' gold rush in social sciences does not necessarily translate into real insights. For instance, the question of real-life quality relationships remains. There are many friends on Facebook. If an employee has to use Facebook for enabling their work relationships and therefore spends most of their Facebook time with co-workers, this does not mean that their family, who might appear less in the social graph, is less important to them. The number of friends in Facebook within a certain group does not imply a strong qualitative relationship. Overall, we are still struggling to develop meaningful models that could make valid conclusions from online behaviour about how people behave outside the web.

The fiercest criticisms of big data were, however, not targeted at its practices that produce a new digital divide, but at the provocations some of its proponents offered about the way big data would waltz away all we thought we knew (Borgman, 2012). In particular, Anderson from the *Wired* magazine had declared the 'end of theory', as he argued:

> This is a world where massive amounts of data and applied mathematics replace every other tool that might be brought to bear. Out with every theory of human behavior, from linguistics to sociology... With enough data, the numbers speak for themselves.
> (C. Anderson, 2008a)

The claim for the 'end of theory' was meant as a provocation and, reading the quote carefully, it is actually the end of some theories (e.g. sociological ones) and the emergence of new ones that can produce the models such as applied mathematics. Nevertheless, even this claim towards the end of certain theories seems exaggerated, at least for the moment.

The 'end of theory' paradigm has been criticised for its examples (Callebaut, 2012), where the numbers just do not speak for themselves, and for its epistemological foundations (Mayer-Schönberger and Cukier, 2013), which seem even worse, as big data itself is founded in theory. There are no facts without theory and therefore also no data, which is one of the illusions of 'raw data'. Much of the disruptive power of big data for traditional fields of enquiry does not stem from giving up on any theory, but from exploring new ways of looking at existing problems, from using new theories that up to now seemed alien to many parts of research (Boyd and Crawford, 2012). Anderson provoked a debate, but his claim only confirmed research as we know it. New models and methodologies emerge and provide new insights. This is hardly the end of theory, but rather a confirmation of its continued importance. The disruptive power of big data will then come from putting theory again to the forefront also in areas that have stopped thinking about its theoretical foundations for a while and have become an enquiry industry based on established methods.

Theory is just one area where we can expect to see some immediate impact of big data developments to established procedures and policies. A new legal and ethical framework is needed to govern the 'changing privacy landscape in the era of big data', as '[l]egislative bodies must also be appropriately educated... and expected to enact laws that protect individuals from discrimination based upon their personal information'

(Schadt, 2012). The most obvious 'social peril of big data' (Bollier and Firestone, 2010) are privacy violations, as big data is commonly done behind the back of the people who produced it in the first place. As Antoinette Rouvroy and Yves Poullet have argued,

> [V]ast collections and intensive processing of data enable data controllers such as governmental authorities or private companies to take decisions about individual subjects on the basis of these collected and processed personal information without allowing for any possibility for the data subjects to know exactly which data would be used...
>
> (Rouvroy and Poullet, 2009: 68)

Big data is often about people, who are good sources of velocity, variety and volume. While we already have working frameworks to ensure ethical behaviour for traditional methods of establishing people's opinions such as surveys or even elections, little has been done up to now to work on a big data ethical environment. Boyd and Crawford (2012) give the example that traditional ethical approval for studies on human behaviour depends on asking for consent of all study participants. In the big data world, this will not be feasible; even standard computational techniques such as anonymisation need to be adapted. Big data offers more opportunities to de-anonymise existing data sets using a combination of related data (Bollier and Firestone, 2010).

Pavolotsky (2012) discusses the many other legal issues big data involves and concludes that many of them are already known from the days when we just had data. Next to privacy concerns, there are those that cover intellectual property rights, where 'the practitioner should consider the entire data life cycle, which consists of data generation, transfer, use, transformation, storage, archival, and destruction' (Pavolotsky, 2012: 3). The nature of the data is here still more critical than the size. Does the data contain information about persons or other kind of security-critical items? Big data also still has a location – at least from the legal point of view. Where the data is stored matters when it comes to assessing legal requirements, as privacy laws differ from country to country (Jaeger et al., 2009). Finally, APIs that give access to big data often come with their own licences. The *New York Times* API, for instance, has detailed instructions to developers (*http://developer.nytimes.com/Api_terms_of_use*). Based on the experience we had with data before the age of big data, a lot of work awaits law practitioners in the future from people, who experience human right abuses from the big data analytics done to them, from software providers who would like to be not involved in the big data analytics of their competitors, to many other new parties (Pavolotsky, 2012).

If we ask for more regulation to make big data comply with basic legal standards and make the analytics more just, governments will most likely be charged to come up with such regulations. Yet governments are big data organisations themselves and public trust in them as honest 'brokers' of big data has been damaged, not least by Snowden's revelations, but also by previous leaks from digital surveillance progammes. Government agencies seem to be the largest big data collectors of all. They are involved in collecting for the sake of collecting. Otherwise, some of their activities cannot be explained, as it is doubtful that some of the collected data, as described by Snowden, can actually lead to any meaningful analysis. Of course, we do not know the full extent of the analytical possibilities of NSA (National Security Agency), GCHQ (Government Communications Headquarters) and others, but we do know the currently accepted limitations of big data analytics. If the *Guardian* big surveillance tracker should be trusted, there are simply too many terabytes involved (Davis et al., 2013). Some of the projects revealed by Snowden seem to go far beyond what is currently possible, but this would be the subject of another investigation.

The government has the advantage that it can collect data from its citizens, often without asking them, as the Snowden affair tells us. Census data is captured every couple of years, ID cards are handed out with exact records of where people live or electoral records for health care are laid down. No other big data organisation can do this, but this also raises suspicions and comparisons with totalitarianism. Comparisons with the Stasi are not far away. The Stasi was the East German state security service that famously collected information on everyone at almost any moment in time. It was its own kind of big data organisation. The Stasi was one of the most feared security agencies of the Eastern bloc, but nowadays smartphones collect more information about their owners than these agencies could have ever dreamt of (Craig and Ludloff, 2011). Stasi records were very comprehensive, but hardly capable to work in real-time; they yielded mainly documents that had not been reduced to the essential data yet. For instance, locations needed to be extracted from these documents. Mobile phones deliver these in a readily reusable data format that can even be easily visualised in any standard map application.

Mayer-Schönberger and Cukier (2013) analyse how the thinking about surveillance becomes datafied itself. Surveillance crowds are summarised by what a computer can learn from them by using their Facebook or mobile phone behaviour (Mayer-Schönberger and Cukier, 2013: 157). People are made legible in terms of the networks in which they are integrated. It becomes important not just to know about this person but, just as the Stasi was interested in discovering the relationships of all their subjects (in the end, of all German Democratic Republic citizens), in the era of big data, government analysts become interested in everything they can find out about a person's friends, the friends of these friends and so on. The Stasi wanted to do this, too, but was limited in how deeply it could draw these graphs. With big data, it has become much easier to expand the depth of relationship knowledge. Then, it also makes sense always to collect data on people and objects that are potentially involved in these relationships. Never mind whether a particular person has already been suspicious or not; in the future, data on them might be part of closing the data graph around a suspect.

We should not be surprised that governments are engaged deeply in such collection activities. After all, we have already agreed that, in exchange for using a free Gmail service, Google can use our datafied desires to offer us new products. Our culture is our currency here. Reeves (2013) analyses how Americans have been enrolled in general surveillance. Unless we want to start paying for services such as Gmail, we cannot stop this. But we need to learn to understand better how big data is used and to be able to opt out if we cannot agree with the usage.

We spoke at the beginning of this chapter about the three Vs that describe big data. All of them lead to new usage and finally to new value creation from the existing content that organisations have at hand. Value has recently been added as the fourth V to the definition of big data (Biehn, 2013). This is a good addition, as indeed big data has led to completely new ideas about value. In particular, we have already mentioned the network value, which we shall investigate now in more detail in our final chapter, where we discuss the impact of crowds and clouds on a changing economy and society.

This chapter started with the difficulties of defining big data after we have met the phenomenon several times throughout this book. Firstly, we specified the difference between data and content and have seen how crowds and clouds help transform big content into big data. Big data is generally described with the three Vs – velocity, variety and volume – and crowds and clouds are key to the production and consumption of big data under each V. The history of big data has finally taught us that the importance of crowds and clouds has always been the case since big data has first been identified in extremely large science work.

Collecting is the digital activity that defines big data, even before all the new analysis that we can do with it. Big data technologies, from NoSQL to MapReduce, have been advanced to support this collecting, and big data organisations have been established to coordinate the collecting between the various involved partners. The gold rush in big data applications has made this clear – not only in social media, but also in retail or government work. But the collecting also generates anxieties about the amount of information collected and how it can be misused to create a new digital authoritarian rule over economy and society.

6

Economy and society of crowds and clouds

Abstract: This chapter discusses some of the economic and social concepts linked to digital ecosystems. Next to the division of work between humans and computers, the new phenomenon of free labour is presented, before we come to the kind of value that really seems to matter in the world of crowds and clouds, which is the network value. It describes how the value of digital assets more and more depends on how deeply they are embedded in the global networks, and how much they motivate other consumers. The network value plays a role in all applications of digital ecosystems that we investigate throughout this book – so much so, that digital assets cannot be discussed any further without considering their network value.

Key words: digital assets and media in economy and society, digital workflows, free labour, network value, division of labour, humans and machines.

The new division of labour between humans and computers

Data and content have become key to the digital economy as a whole, as seen in the examples of Apple's iTunes or Netflix. As boundary objects, they often link separate systems together and are central to the overall business strategy. In this chapter, we do not want simply to repeat the message that media and other digital assets play an important role within the future digital economy, but to look beyond the current hype and investigate some of the major challenges and criticisms that the new digital ecosystem-based economy faces. We draw on several concepts that have traditionally been used to engage critically with economic development and analyse what kind of role these concepts might play in the economy of digital ecosystems. We firstly investigate the new emerging division of labour between humans and computers, and tackle the question of what alienation might be in this new division of labour. Secondly, we investigate the contribution of free labour to the digital economy, before turning to the new emerging type of network value in the final section of this chapter.

We started discussing the division of labour in the digital ecosystem in Chapter 2. We argued that the digital ecosystem is governed by a peculiar mixture of crowds, which inhabit clouds. 'Cloud' is a generic name we have used to summarise all kinds of technological platforms. The new platform technologies have developed much faster than anyone could have imagined (see Chapter 3). They also push existing organisational and legal frameworks to the limit (again, see Chapter 3). In this chapter, we take a deeper look into the societal and economic conditions that are built around it.

One of the early major works on the new division of labour between humans and computers was *The New Division of Labor: How Computers Are Creating the Next Job Market* by Frank Levy and Richard J. Murnane (2012). Originally published in 2004, the book is now partly outdated, but its general insight that the future economy will be determined by the successful division of labour between humans and computers is even more relevant today in the era of big data, as new economic models are envisaged, away from Wall Street and towards Silicon Valley. Digital asset and media management is here just one example among many.

Levy and Murnane's book is still relevant, as it explores a larger trend. At the beginning of the book, the authors refer to the 1964 Lyndon Johnson Commission report on the division of work between humans and machines and state that 'computers now replace humans in carrying out an ever widening range of tasks... And beyond directly replacing humans, computers have become the infrastructure of the global economy, helping jobs move quickly to sources of cheap labor' (Levy and Murnane, 2012: 1). But they also believe that many cognitive tasks are immune from possible computerisation; they have in mind creative tasks such as the classification of multimedia assets and recommend looking at the whole economy, rather than individual business processes, to understand how the new division of labour works (Mansell, 2004).

With their exemptions, the authors sometimes go too far and underestimate the dynamics of a modern digital ecosystem. Nowadays, it includes increasingly those aspects of work life that formerly required face-to-face communication, which Levy and Murnane thought to be exempt from computerisation. They could not foresee the emergence of collective digital intelligence and new forms of human-to-human communications that the social web has made possible. This chapter will also show how every aspect of life can be integrated into computer work now, as the digital ecosystem includes the crowds. For instance, one of Levy and Murnane's examples of things computers could never do includes recommendations for childcare. However, it is not outrageous to assume that today we trust online reviews of nannies for our children more than we trust the recommendation by a neighbour. Computers have not replaced the human labour, but have simply integrated it using the collective intelligence of the social web.

Levy and Murnane point to the new challenges of this new division of labour between humans and the universal machines that are computers, but they also see the opportunities that arise from these associations. This is what their most famous predecessors of the industrial age also did. Adam Smith and other early political economists first discussed the modern revolution implied by a division of labour between humans and machines (A. Smith, 1999). The new division of labour cannot be understood without finding out about its origins in its earlier, industrial forms. This is what we would like to discuss briefly next.

Many consider the systematic development of division of labour as one of the turning points in history. Historically speaking, the division of labour has always attempted to enhance individual skills and possibilities, and reorganise them in order to make the final product larger than the sum of its parts. The father of political economy, Adam Smith, considered growth and increasing wealth of the nations to be rooted in the division of labour. Large jobs are broken down into smaller ones, which can be more easily and more efficiently done and distributed among a larger community. Machines play a decisive role here. In the days of Smith, these were the early mainly mechanical machines and steam engines. Today, this role is played by the universal machine: the computer. What do we mean by a 'universal machine'? The computer is a universal machine, as it can do any task it is programmed to. It is not limited to a single or a number of tasks that were hard-wired into machines before it. An ecosystem based on steam engines would be impossible.

Adam Smith (1999: 120) argued that machines need to be considered as tools that help increase the potential of individual workers and enhance their physical and mental abilities. Progress in science and technology then always leads to liberation of labour and to more sophisticated means of production. But Smith identified a number of problems of machines that take over the interesting aspects of work life. Just like Karl Marx after him, Smith already saw the potential of a division of labour that could lead to an 'alienation' of the individual from the products of labour and a dissatisfied workforce. Smith believed the answer to be improved education of the workers in order to provide them with better life opportunities. The alienation of individuals from their own products of work has since become one of the strongest critical concerns about the division of labour.

Marx famously went beyond Smith in his critique of alienation that might develop out of modern work processes (Marx, 1867). He insisted that education cannot be the answer to overcome alienation. Marx agreed with Smith on the potentially liberating effects of advancements in science and technology. However, for him, machinery as a result of technological progress liberated not humans, but capital and its process of value creation. The history of capitalism has shown that the process of capital runs more effectively as machinery reaches further. For Marx, capitalist machinery was a system, not just a tool to optimise work processes in order to extract more value. As he always considered the role of society as well, this also implies that machinery has an important, if not the most important, role in organising society as a whole by integrating all work processes in it. In fact, he already used organic metaphors in order to describe this system, which makes him a predecessor of modern thinking about digital ecosystems. For instance, Marx's organic composition of capital describes the relationship of machinery and human capital invested to make a profit.

As seen for Marx and Smith, alienation traditionally problematises the position of the creators of value in the context of a division of work between humans and machines. In many ways, we have not moved much beyond this discussion on the value of machinery for the liberation of the human, even now as we have entered the digital economy and its related ecosystems. As we shall see later on, some observers point to the development of new digital precarious work governed by computer processes, while others emphasise the liberation of labour in what is called the knowledge economy and commons-based peer productions. But the division itself is hardly ever discussed. With the advent of the digital economy, we can, however, observe a fundamental shift in this division, which also explains why alienation as category of critique might be insufficient. The digital ecosystem sees free, commons-based labour as well as a new form of networked value emerging, which we shall discuss later in this chapter. In order to question some of these developments and their impact on human society, one needs to start from these new concepts, unknown to traditional political economy – at least in the context of value production.

The emerging digital economy, which we witness growing around us, is difficult to define. Many authors who discuss it only seem to know for sure that there is a fundamental shift in the means of production going on. Wall Street and Silicon Valley stand without doubt for the two coining industries of the early twenty-first century. As foreseen by Levy and Murnane, computers define the infrastructure for both types of industries. Both are heavily digitally organised and have developed their specific work practices between humans and computers that support their apparent success. The finance industry amasses huge amounts of data to help it measure the risks of its investments, while Silicon Valley is famous for its own working culture that enables creative work involved in software asset production to flourish. At the same time, Silicon Valley manages to maintain a high level of management expertise.

Wall Street and Silicon Valley are very different in their structures, but both recognise the value of the new digital networks. Based on digital technologies, both industries have developed multinational digital ecosystems that created highly interdependent work processes across continents. Digital asset management is following the lead of these two industries in integrating ever more complex human–machine workflows. For digital asset management, we are only beginning to see these globally interconnected workflows emerging.

The ever more complex workflows of (digital) asset and content management in global industries have not gone unnoticed. Brynjolfsson and McAfee quote supply-chain information asset management:

> For instance, companies like CVS have embedded processes like prescription drug ordering into their enterprise information systems. Each time CVS makes an improvement, it is propagated across 4,000 stores nationwide, amplifying its value. As a result, the reach and impact of an executive decision, like how to organize a process, is correspondingly larger.
>
> (Brynjolfsson and McAfee, 2011: 640)

However, hardly anyone investigates these workflows for their impact on the digital worker involved in them, which is the question behind alienation. Michael McNally (2010) is one of the few exceptions we could find. He analyses how enterprise content management systems streamline digital production processes, and how this leads to disastrous effects on intellectual workers. They are alienated from their digital product in the Smithian and Marxian sense: 'Content management systems deskill workers by subdividing intellectual tasks into the smallest possible constituent parts and automating as many tasks as possible' (McNally, 2010: 357).

McNally goes against the general theory, also repeated in this book, that content management systems enrich the life of digital work by reducing the number of boring repetitive tasks. He agrees that this might also be the case, but for him they are mainly management tools, which reduce the digital worker's creative influence on the end results of production. This is a strong assumption, which is important to explore further, as it can lead us to a critique of labour processes in digital content and asset management.

In order to underline his critique, McNally effectively equates modern workflow systems with traditional conveyor belts that forced workers to repeat the same tasks over and over again. He uses the metaphor of the Fordist assembly lines to describe content management processes: '[A]utomation and Fordist assembly lines were the implements of the degradation of physical/industrial work in the twentieth century. The same potential for the degradation of intellectual labour in the twenty-first century is present in enterprise content management systems' (McNally, 2010: 367). However, he goes too far in equating digital workflow systems with conveyor belts. Although he is right to emphasise that modern workflows, not just in the digital industries, partly prevent the digital worker from taking ownership of the whole process, they are about so much more than that. Workflow systems (Deelman et al., 2009) were originally developed to return control of a flow into the hands of those who manage it or those who execute it rather than the masters of the digital universe, the programmers. They are simple ways of bringing together services that do not require programming expertise. This remains their principal aim, even if they can be used in content management systems to monitor and control work processes. McNally seems to ignore this aspect.

He rightly notes that the control in content management applications is not the result of the technology alone, but also of how it is used. He then, however, lists mainly features from some of the main providers of content management systems to present his criticism. Unfortunately, his analysis falls short of the discussion of the interlinkage of human and computer labour, through which he might have been able to show in more detail a critique of work relationships that he assumes dominate digital content and asset management. His criticism is based on alienation, which seems not to be enough, as workflows and their systems cannot be compared to traditional conveyor belts. They are an expression of the fact that computers are universal machines. In order to understand better the transformation that takes place here, it is good to go back to the general development of the interlinkage of human and computers. We need to look beyond theories of alienation and investigate how humans and computers are interdependent in a global workflow.

As seen, alienation is founded in the division of labour according to Marx and Smith. McNally's adoption of its critical potential for analysing digital content work processes assumes that this division of labour has not essentially changed with the advent of a new type of machine, the computer. His problems in identifying a digital workflow engine with a means to control the digital content workers indicate that this is not the case, and that the division of labour between human and computers is principally different from earlier ones between traditional machines and computers. This has become clear in the analysis by Levy and Murnane (2012), as discussed earlier.

A more recent publication takes up this theme of the division of labour and alienation: *Race Against the Machine: How the Digital Revolution is Accelerating Innovation, Driving Productivity, and Irreversibly Transforming Employment and the Economy* by Erik Brynjolfsson and Andrew McAfee (2011). Brynjolfsson is widely recognised for his contributions to the idea of a long-tail economy, which is the foundation of many of the new value assumptions in the digital economy (Brynjolfsson et al., 2006). The long tail implies that, with the web, it becomes easier to sell a large number of unique items to until now unknown customers, as the distribution and marketing for these assets becomes so much easier. Anderson popularised this concept in his book *The Long Tail: Why the Future of Business Is Selling Less of More* (C. Anderson, 2008b), where he also cites Brynjolfsson's study. With the web, any niche consumption can all of a sudden become profitable.

Because the web makes it cheap to distribute digital content assets, even items generally in low demand can make a profit. Based on research by Brynjolfsson et al. (2010), Anderson argues that Amazon has shown how to make money also from books that could not be sold in traditional bookstores, as demand for them is not high enough. In this sense, the long tail prepares Brynjolfsson's and McAfee's later work on the new work relationships emerging for the digital economy. They relate the use of computers to the general race with machines that human work processes are exposed to, but, contrary to McNally, they take into consideration what distinguishes computers from traditional machines.

Through the media focus on the financial crisis and the problems of the finance industries, what seems to have gone unnoticed is how other parts of the digital economy have led to massive shifts in the work relationships of humans and computers in the past decade. The change relates to the substitution of human labour with computer labour and the authors of *Race Against the Machine* are worried that the 'median worker' is left behind and computers will result not in a more equal society but in a fundamentally more divided one. Computers seem to replace human labour on an ever faster and larger scale, and they seem to be very good at it, with no end in sight.

Digital asset management itself is an example. Here, the task of classifying items, which was done in traditional (digital) library environments by clerks or data officers, is now done by computer machines relying on key words in asset descriptions in order to classify these assets. This is not always perfect, but it is at least consistent. Digital asset management workflows are automated on an ever-increasing scale. In the overall economy, computers seem to replace what have previously been considered to be uniquely human activities. Data, digital content and digital assets have played a key role in allowing computers to reach out to new areas of the work process that seemed to be the exclusive domain of the human until very recently. Some claim that data and digital content have replaced processing power as the new driver in the development of the digital economy. Data is the new 'Intel Inside', as Tim O'Reilly has called it, and has become one of the principles of his Web 2.0 manifesto (O'Reilly, 2007).

One of the best examples of the increased power of digital assets and data comes from Brynjolfsson and McAfee themselves. Their 2011 book is based on the analysis by Levy and Murnane, and the latter pair's examples of the general limits of the substitution of human labour by computers. Among these examples was one that Brynjolfsson and McAfee especially argue against. For Levy and Murnane, computers will never be able to drive cars by themselves. Brynjolfsson and McAfee, however, can point towards Google Streetcar (Brynjolfsson and McAfee, 2011), which has shown that computers can be safe and effective drivers (though still in limited circumstances). Google Streetcar has solved this impossibility not because it is the perfected artificial intelligence whose reasoning is close to the human's in street traffic, but because Google Streetcar can rely on data collected for Google Maps and Google Street View that datafied traffic behaviour. Thus many possible situations for cars in traffic had already been recorded in Google's vast data stores and there is no need for renewed reasoning when the Google Streetcar finally passes the same street.

Data is truly the new 'Intel Inside' for the Streetcar, and, as already noted, Marissa Mayer, Google's former VP of Search Products and User Experience, confessed to InfoWorld 'that having access to large amounts of data is in many instances more important than creating great algorithms' (Perez, 2007). It is not just the data assets in Google's store that enable the Streetcar to drive automatically. It is only through the contribution of millions of users and their analyses of streets and places that the computerised car will be prepared to deal with the traffic. This additional information to the original data assets contributed by millions makes the car drive. The rest is artificial intelligence-based algorithmic reasoning, now made easier by the big data assets that Google has, enriched by real user experiences. Google uses their free labour, a concept we shall return to later in this chapter.

In order to overcome what computers can and cannot do, it seems key that human intelligence is integrated into their reasoning of big data. New tasks such as driving a car have not been done by computers alone; they have been done by computers embedded within a strong digital ecosystem that has brought together the collective intelligence of its human and computer agents, recorded in rich data assets. Therefore, for Brynjolfsson and McAfee, digitisation is a process of 'creative destruction' (Brynjolfsson and McAfee, 2011: 340), used to redefine the existing relationship between machines and humans. With computers, this relationship has changed forever, as the human general-purpose machine is now met by another general-purpose machine – the computer. This implies, however, that the challenge of machines for human labour has grown as human labour has become even more universally substitutable.

According to Brynjolfsson and McAfee, creativity cannot be embedded in the assembly lines of the early twentieth century that traditional theories of alienation targeted. Creativity emerged in the scientific-technological innovation outside the production lines and was then materialised in them. Computers go beyond this schema, as they can be changed at almost any moment in time. In a world where computers are production machines, innovation is now part of work processes themselves. Brynjolfsson and McAfee see computers as the bearers of great opportunities. Given that innovation can be embedded in computing machines, humans can win the race not by competing against them, but by competing alongside them. Finally, Brynjolfsson and McAfee argue that '[t]he solution is organizational innovation: co-inventing new organizational structures, processes, and business models that leverage ever-advancing technology and human skills' (Brynjolfsson and McAfee, 2011: 186). Contrary to McNally's analysis, in this approach, workflow systems that help embed human labour would be part of the solution rather than part of the problem.

Chess is one of the favourite examples that Brynjolfsson and McAfee provide in order to demonstrate new successful ways of competing with machines. By now, the best chess player in the world is not a human or a computer alone, but a human–computer combination. The best chess is played combining the processing power of computers with the imagination of humans. These kinds of productive partnerships are being formed everywhere. The process of attaching semantics to assets is still a task reserved in large parts to humans, in particular considering complex multimedia assets. But computers can support this process effectively by narrowing the choices. The open-source digital asset management system Nuxeo, for instance, has successfully integrated the Apache Stanbol semantic services platform (Behrendt, 2012). The platform supports the process of annotating digital assets with metadata and delivers new digital asset links to outside contextual resources. The computer work is still supervised by a human, but has the advantage of providing more consistent metadata than a human annotator would on their own. Nuxeo and others put their hope here not just in the professional metadata exploitation of their own crowds, but in the belief that that experts in their own digital assets will contribute voluntarily and add their own free labour.

Free and collective labour

We have seen that a traditional analysis of division of labour has limitations when it comes to investigating the digital ecosystem. The concepts of alienation due to the division of labour cannot explain the dynamic character of the division of labour in a digital ecosystem based on the interaction between humans and computers. Another characteristic of the current digital ecosystem is the voluntary contribution of human labour, which can hardly be imagined for large-scale production of assets in the Fordist assembly line.

Therefore, we would now like to investigate how free labour is integrated into the digital ecosystem and later on how it contributes to a new type of value, which we call 'network value'. Free labour, or the voluntary contribution of effort, is another difficult concept for traditional political economy. The question is: how can this kind of voluntary labour contribute value to a product? We shall see that in the digital ecosystem, free labour is essential for new network value, as only with this can a digital asset be effectively positioned within the digital ecosystem.

For our nineteenth-century political economists Marx and Smith, the contribution of free labour to value production is difficult to apprehend. Smith famously stated:

> ... the real price of every thing, what really costs to the man who wants to acquire it, is the toil and trouble of acquiring it. What every thing is really worth to the man who has acquired it, and who wants to dispose of it or exchange it for something else, is the toil and trouble which it can save to himself, and which it can impose upon other people.
>
> (Smith, quoted in Dupre and Gagnier, 1996: 553)

Smith goes on to say that labour is the name for all this trouble. Free labour, on the other hand, assumes that there is no real trouble involved in the production. It is as pleasurable as drinking water was for Smith, only it has value for someone. Marx agrees on the hardships of value production and that labour run by capital is the only one that produces value. This assumes that the labourer has sold their labour force in exchange for the means of living, something that does also not really happen with free labour. It seems that for Marx, too, the concept of value-producing free labour is difficult to understand.

Of course, objective definitions of value such as those of Marx and Smith seem outdated today, but even subjective definitions of value need to assume that some kind of formal exchange takes place before something can have value. In the age of social media, this exchange has accelerated, is deeply embedded in everyday actions and is not noted any more. There is most likely no contractual relationship that binds free labour to a digital product. Everyone can and is supposed to produce digital media and content. Labour is added freely and the result of the production is based on a flexible combination of free and paid labour.

Nowadays, digital labour is almost always also based on what has aptly been called 'commons-based peer-production' (Benkler and Nissenbaum, 2006). This especially dominates the new digital media world, where it is often the main type of production, as in the case of social media sites such as YouTube or Facebook.

Benkler sees fundamental transformations taking place, which will lead to:

> ... substantial redistribution of power and money from the twentieth-century industrial producers of information, culture, and communications – like Hollywood, the recording industry, and perhaps the broadcasters and some of the telecommunications services giants – to a combination of widely diffuse populations around the globe, and the market actors that will build the tools that make this population better able to produce its own information environment rather than buying it ready-made.
>
> (Benkler, 2006: 23)

This is the optimistic view where consumers of digital media are also their producers. Peer production is supposed to have a liberating effect and is celebrated.

Others see a darker side, too. Andrejevic aims to develop a theory of exploitation in the digital era for what he calls the interactive economy. Free labour is used to build up 'online community and sociality upon privately controlled network infrastructures' (Andrejevic, 2009: 419). In the enthusiasm for free labour, it is sometimes forgotten that exploitation and adverse working conditions are still very much part of the digital economy. Exploitation has been part of the global digital economy from its very beginnings. The digital ecosystem promises to integrate the remote workforce easily, be it computers or humans. In the case of citizen cyber-science, this can be celebrated as a contribution to the higher good of science, as we have seen in Chapter 3. But the easy availability of any remote workforce has also got a more problematic dimension. Exploitation is at hand, too.

Julian Dibbell (2007) gives an early example. He reports in the *New York Times* on the work of Li Qiwen, who made a living from playing the online game World of Warcraft night after night. In the game, he collected virtual currency gold coins, which were then sold online for real money to real gamers in Europe and America. Using this virtual currency, gamers can immediately buy new equipment for the game or advance to new levels in World of Warcraft without the hassle of collecting gold themselves. Furthermore, just like in real gold rushes, the big money is not made by Li Qiwen, but by the intermediaries who trade the gold online. In 2007, when Dibbell wrote this article, the worldwide trade in such types of digital assets was an estimated US$1.8 billion. Since then, it has grown strongly and new games are now sold with built-in options to pay a little extra for better weapons, more skills, etc. that help with the gameplay.

Nowhere, however, does the exploitation of remote workforces become more obvious than in the dominating commercial crowd environment, Amazon's Mechanical Turk. Fort (2011) asks whether the 'dream come true' of 'hobby workers' supporting global digital production has become sour and the Turk's 'gold mine' is in truth a 'coal mine'. Leisure and hobby are seldom the reason why Turk workers stick with it:

> The observed mean hourly wages for performing jobs in the MTurk system is below US$ 2. However, money is an important motivation for a majority of the Turkers (20% use MTurk as their primary source of income, and 50% as their secondary source of income), and leisure is important for only a minority (30%).
>
> (Fort, 2011)

Basic other rights also seem to disappear quickly in the global crowd. There is, for instance, no guarantee of payment after the job and there are no benefits. *http://turkernation.com* has a hall of shame of worst jobs for Turkers.

Ross et al. (2010) analyse the changing demographics after Amazon had changed its general payment policies for Turkers. Workers come now more and more from countries outside the USA, mainly from India. Furthermore, they participate not in order to kill time and enjoy themselves, but to earn money as their primary or secondary source of income. Once professionalised, Turkers have also attracted activists, who try to make the invisible Turkers visible. Irani and Silberman (2013), for instance, present their system Turkopticon, which is essentially a browser extension that allows workers to evaluate their relationship to the Mechanical Turk employers and share this evaluation with others.

While nowadays Turkers have become professionalised and are not involved in peer production, it is still true that most of the work in what Andrejevic has called 'digital sociality' is based on free labour and voluntary contribution. In this sociality, the consumers of digital media are not supposed to find out that they have also become producers, which makes it so difficult to understand how they add value. The digital media consumers are not aware that they are part of the production process if, for instance, they post a video to YouTube (Deuze, 2009). The follow-on question by Deuze (2009) is how we can discuss production and consumption of digital media, when most of the current processes around these seem to include both aspects. The closure of the logical layers of the web ensures that all user activities in relation to social media are included in the production of digital media assets.

Deuze (2008) cites 'upstream marketing', which targets customer needs by making use of complex digital analysis methods to capture the 'productive' user behaviour, as well as their attitudes towards digital media products. This analysis is then used to create new digital media products. Media in general and digital social media in particular is a globally interconnected business (Deuze, 2008), which is dominated by global workflows that incorporate complex patterns of outsourcing and inclusion, but that are at the same time clustered at particular places and global centres of media.

Digital media assets lend themselves to allowing the user to be actively involved in the production and deeply embedded in social media workflows. Next to upstream marketing, O'Reilly (2007) cites the production of games, where consumers have quickly become co-producers. He also makes the important point that the media industries' ecosystem is not just set up to support the production of digital content, but also the platforms that allow for the production of digital assets (such as content management or digital asset management systems) and allow for connectivity between consumers and producers.

> As argued before, in the current digital and networked global media ecosystem the roles played by advertisers, media producers and content consumers are converging... The production system of the media industry is a case in point, as it has become networked on a 'translocal' scale, integrating different locales of cultural production into a global production system, integrating and localizing cultural values and regional symbols across dispersed markets.
>
> (Deuze, 2009: 473)

Deuze lays out how Benkler's commons-based peer production is at least partly the result of a drive by (social) media industries, which target free labour. In the new digital economy, the distinction between free labour and official media and content producers is characterised by complex overlaps.

Digital media management in the television industry is here just one example among many. Fish (2011) analyses the use of free labour for digital asset management in the production of novel TV shows. His subject of study is the Current TV production, a US-based TV station, founded by the former US presidential candidate Al Gore. Current TV got into the news again in 2013, when it was dissolved and sold to Al Jazeera, allowing the organisation to broadcast on US networks for the first time. Current TV's stated aim was to publish the work of citizen journalists to provide content that would report directly from the daily life of people. In this way, Al Gore hoped to foster the democratic engagement of young people (Fish, 2011).

Subsequently, Current TV created a programme called Viewer-Created Content (VC2). 'In competitive businesses (media production) or difficult situations (refugee camps) locating individuals might be easier than training them up to standards that would eliminate the need for the management firms' (Fish, 2011: 470). All that was needed to maintain this programme was a small number of central staff who controlled the outsourced work and managed the incoming digital media assets, programmers and information specialists. VC2 did not pay a minimum wage, but aimed to provide a valuable experience to many digital content producers and consumers. VC2 was finally abolished in 2008, as the quality of the content was often not good enough, and problems with intellectual property occurred frequently in this form of digital outsourcing.

As previously discussed, social media companies in the wider sense of the word, which would also include Current TV, try to create an ecosystem around them and rely on free labour and other contributions to develop their platform. For companies, engagement with free labour from consumers and others promises a deeper involvement with their products. Those like Current TV, who sell digital media assets, are not the only enthusiasts for free labour. It begins earlier in the process, as the various open-source DAM (digital asset management) systems show. The production of digital asset management systems targets free labour more and more as a useful source to produce and enhance digital assets. Open-source business models for DAM providers are naturally closely linked to employing the power of peer production.

Garzarelli et al. (2008) think that opening source and content will help with market expansion more quickly, because of the open division of labour that is enabled by them. They realise the promises of the crowd. In open content environments, the best-suited individuals for a particular task can be easily found among professional and non-professional peers, or between ‘closed’ and free labour. Garzarelli et al. (2008) contrast what they call cathedral production of proprietary licences with the bazaar-type production based on open licences. ‘In essence’, they argue, ‘the difference between the two ideal types is that one is a top-down, centralized organization, while the other is a bottom-up, decentralized organization in which information is horizontally spread’ (Garzarelli et al., 2008: 9). Bazaar-type production caters for active participation by users where they can pick and choose the pieces to which they would like to contribute. The similarities to the definition of the crowd (Malone et al., 2009) in Chapter 2 are obvious.

In the cathedral-type production, employees are hired according to dedicated specialisations. Coding, for instance, is clearly separated from specification tasks, which in turn requires detailed planning. This kind of production has recently become outdated, as the development of digital assets has been increasingly vertically integrated. Bazaar production, on the other hand, relies on collective intelligence and, most importantly, also on the free labour of all the participants in the development process. Tasks are taken up by those interested in them (Garzarelli et al., 2008) and can therefore also be done by volunteers. Potentially, this leads to productive economies of redundancies, as various developers will try the same task.

Nuxeo is one of those companies that have developed a complex open-source DAM system. They wagered that bazaar-type production for an open-source DAM system, which allows for professional and non-professional contributions, would develop a deeper trust relationship with the customers and easier ways to embed the systems directly into existing customer workflows. As in most cases, the ‘free labour’ that constitutes the digital commons sphere is based, in this case, on paid-for-work by Nuxeo. The open-source community has moved away from being driven by a couple of after-work hackers that make it their hobby to programme Linux distributions. It has developed into a community driven by people who work for companies or institutions that decide to make their source code freely available on the bazaar.

Corporate open source is therefore an expression of the tension of closeness and openness in digital ecosystems, as ‘ideas can be shared and owned, credited and appropriated, open and proprietary at the same time’ (Newfield, 2013: 6). Charges apply ‘through the platform’ that the crowds want to use. A good example for this change in open-source production is the open-source digital asset management system called DuraSpace. Here, public grant money has been used to deliver the core system. While the main focus was initially on serving communities in public services, nowadays DuraSpace has a wide range of commercial applications as a platform for digital asset management and charges for the use of its platform.

Benkler and Nissenbaum's comparison of open-source software and content production with traditional village practices now appears outdated. They state that 'free and open source software development' can be seen as a modern form of 'barn raising – a collective effort of individuals contributing towards a common goal in a more-or-less informal and loosely structured way' (Benkler and Nissenbaum, 2006: 395). Free software might still be produced in such a free collectivist manner, but open-source production has been integrated into mainstream economic processes for a while now and cannot be compared to barn raising. Open source targets free labour from the production process of the digital asset management systems to the consumption of digital media assets. It makes it easier to produce network values, which can only work in open, interoperable systems.

Network value

Not every digital media and content asset can be raised like a barn. Only some can be produced by dividing their production processes into smaller units, which can then be distributed among free labour. Commonly quoted counter-examples include large and labour-intensive intellectual products such as the writing of novels. But other forms of data sets can also be difficult to produce. Every digital asset can, however, benefit from additional information that can support its value. We call this the network effort that easily occurs in commons-based peer production systems. It comes naturally where peers work together. This network value is the next category we would like to investigate in this chapter.

With free labour, companies hope for network effects around their digital products. We have seen in Chapter 5 how Google, for instance, exploits its advanced access to information needs of search crowds to promote its prediction capacities. Companies, in general, hope to generate one of the most important values in the digital ecosystem, the network value. 'Network value is a reflection of the benefits associated with a large cohort of fellow adopters (installed base) for the product, whereas network-independent value represents benefits conferred by inherent, physical attributes embodied in each unit of the good' (McIntyre and

Subramaniam, 2009: 1496). This is not to be confused with the value of the network itself (its size, number of relationships, etc.), for which we have relatively stable measures in different domains (G. Jung and Lee, 2010). The idea of network value is more related to Bourdieu's structuralist attempt to define the value of an element by the range of relationships the element is embedded in, and within what he calls a 'field' – a specific social setting like a political or economic organisation (Kauppi, 2003).

Marx and Smith would disagree with the second description by McIntyre and Subramaniam (2009) of network-independent value, but then the first type of value, the network value, was completely unknown to them. Free labour helps develop and maintain this large 'installed base' of consumers and producers of a digital asset. In this way, the products a company owns become an essential part of the overall ecosystem, without which the whole system could not function any more. The company behind them becomes indispensable. In this sense, open-source digital asset management systems target this network value by allowing these systems to be deeply embedded in production processes, while new networks can more easily develop in the noisy bazaar rather than the quiet cathedral.

For computing applications, the network value was first defined by Domingos and Richardson as the target for all data mining applications in marketing. 'We propose to model also the customer's network value: the expected profit from sales to other customers she may influence to buy, the customers those may influence, and so on recursively' (Domingos and Richardson, 2001: 57). Here, the question is who best to target with marketing activities. In the social media world, these will be not just those customers who will purchase a particular product. Next to these, there are those who motivate others to buy and have therefore a large network value. Targeting these with marketing investments can therefore be justified beyond the pure value of selling a particular product.

The challenge is how to quantify this network value, which is much more difficult than valuing those direct values Smith and Marx were talking about. It potentially depends on the whole network, which is the reason why Domingos and Richardson (2001) develop a model to represent the market as a network and model it in a mathematical system. They finally apply the model to a use case from media asset management for marketing films. They improve film marketing by mining social network models from a collaborative filtering repository for films. In the future (Domingos and Richardson, 2001), imagine mining not just as one repository of opinions but a whole range of them, distributed on the Internet.

Pasquinelli (2009), who analyses Google's PageRank algorithm, is critical of network value. PageRank famously ranks websites according to the incoming and outgoing links and therefore attaches a type of network value (or rather authority) to all websites. For Pasquinelli, PageRank is:

> not simply an apparatus of surveillance or control, but a machine to capture living time and living labour and to transform the common intellect into network value. Dataveillance is then made possible only thanks to a monopoly of data that are previously accumulated through the PageRank algorithm.
>
> (Pasquinelli, 2009: 153)

This statement is problematic in many ways. First of all, it offers a rather reductive view of the PageRank algorithm itself and ignores its history and relationship with other attempts to analyse and present web content to users. The structure of the websites is just part of the value Google attaches to them. Contrary to what Pasquinelli (2009) suggests, it is not a value in itself but one in relation to the underlying value, as is, for instance, noted in Domingos and Richardson (2001), where the network value only appears in relation to traditional marketing calculations on value. For Google, the value of a website comes not from itself, but from the marketing it can do with its content. Fulfilling a user's search needs has therefore become a gigantic marketing machine using a combination of algorithmic power and common intellect of the crowds who link items in the digital ecosystem.

Network value helps sell more of the same. A product choice is directly affected by the community surrounding the digital content asset (McIntyre and Subramaniam, 2009). Users want the same things that other members of their crowds want. 'To put it differently, network effects occur when the value of a product or service to a consumer is contingent on the number of other people using it' (ibid.: 1494). The strategies for generating a strong network value is an early focus on a large and stable 'installed base' (McIntyre and Subramaniam, 2009), which implies a strong early adopter community.

Finally, there are indirect network values, which stem from the choice of a platform for digital content. The choice of the cloud will affect the potential network value. The shape of a chair has proven difficult to change once it reached its currently accepted form. The crowd supporting the current way of realising the sitting platform is too strong. In the digital world, one of the most famous examples is the Microsoft Office platform, which has shown to be highly competitive against any new office platform, even though the new ones have exhibited many more advanced features or were simply much cheaper. Platforms have a high network value if they become indispensable for any kind of application and create a de facto standard in an application field, just as Microsoft Word documents have become a universally accepted way of exchanging documents.

With the rise of the network value and the necessary investments to establish it, other costs decrease in importance. Transaction costs, for instance, fall rapidly in the digital ecosystem, which changes the traditional relationship between transactional costs and number of assets produced. While traditionally, the cost of transactions rises exponentially the fewer assets are produced, this does not have to be the case for digital assets. As Ulieru and Verdon (2009) have shown for the case of books distribution by Amazon, transactional costs remain almost constant once a digital infrastructure is in place.

Ulieru and Verdon are particularly interested in the 20/80 per cent rule of thumb, which states that 80 per cent of the effects stem from 20 per cent of the causes. The network value aims to promote these 20 per cent. Traditional knowledge commons projects, such as Linux or Wikipedia, focus not just on experts who can provide specialised knowledge and can deliver a range of products effectively, but also on those who can write about or develop just one specific product. It would be impossible for large physical production processes to hire people and expertise for just one job on the large scale. These items only become interesting once the network value is targeted.

For Ulieru and Verdon, only an architecture of participation, such as the ones for Wikipedia and Linux, helps locate the right expert for any small job and increase the network value:

> We will have to enable a type of personnel platform where each individual's passions, interests, talents, expertise are made available to the whole organization and where the individual can choose to contribute his abilities... We name this organizational platform architecture of participation.
>
> (Ulieru and Verdon, 2009: 21)

Open standards and an architecture of participation clearly lead to higher network value and better 'complementary products' (McIntyre and Subramaniam, 2009) for an ever-increasing crowd, as no interest or product is too small. A product like the iPhone has also attracted a large user base, as it leveraged the power of the crowd to develop new, complementary use of its platform. On the other hand, proprietary formats help protect against competitors. As seen, it has been part of Apple's success story that they were able to mix both approaches successfully. 'Creating an ecosystem of complementors that selectively benefit a particular product can unleash the power of network intensity for competitive advantage' (McIntyre and Subramaniam, 2009: 1512).

Complementors increase digital value, but they do not affect the production of value. The means to organise and manage digital assets is not distributed. The crowd is welcome to enhance the digital asset production process and its value by allowing for easy access and consumption, as well as by adding complementary value to them. It does not produce its own clouds, however. These are in the hands of those with the resources to maintain them. They can be public clouds, such as the Internet Archive, or completely private, like as the ones of Amazon. Both are out of the hands of the crowds who supported the production of digital content. To work 'with a proprietary platform over which the great majority of the players have no control' (Newfield, 2013: 5) is the fate of most free and open labour. Those who own the clouds direct the flow of digital content. Among the big data organisations, discussed in the previous chapter, they are the most powerful in the long term.

This means that, ultimately, the digital ecosystem is also the story of how to take control again in the age of production of digital content and media assets. The digital ecosystem is a 'techno-social system, where peer-production dominates and leadership emerges' (Ulieru and Verdon, 2009: 17). It is about controlling the flow and setting the boundaries of peer production to control the network value. Some thought the Internet, as a peer-based network, would bring about an end to the traditional exchange of social goods, as sustained ownership of digital goods seems to be so much more difficult to keep. Digital goods can be copied easily and the means of their production seem to be distributed. Those who have thought that this would forever change property-based production and render it impossible in the digital economy have forgotten that the Internet is not the web. The web, as described in Chapter 3, is a set of protocols and standards for the interchange of information and digital content. Today's drivers of the digital ecosystem have understood that you can set a cloud on top of the Internet, which can ensure that this interchange does not get out of their control and stays within a controlled digital space, a digital ecosystem with defined virtual borders.

Using this insight that the web and its associated networks can be divided in multiple ways, the big web companies have engaged in new battles for dominance of divisions of the web. In 'Another game of thrones – technology giants at war', the *Economist* (2012) describes how the technology giants Google, Apple, Facebook and Amazon are 'at each other's throats in all sorts of ways'. Apart from Apple, all tech giants are still run by high-profile and very competitive founders, and each has unprecedented financial resources:

> Google has turned search into a huge money-spinner by tying it to advertising. Facebook is in the process of doing something similar with the way people's interests and relationships are revealed by their social networks. Amazon has made it cheap and easy to order physical goods and digital content online. And Apple has minted money by selling beautiful gadgets at premium prices.
>
> (Economist, 2012)

The battlefields between the big four are numerous and are all about making the own ecosystem dominate others in various digital growth markets. There is, first of all, the emerging mobile ecosystem, which has seen software companies transform themselves into hardware companies. Devices for media consumption as much as operating systems, as the lowest levels of virtualisation, are now part of this global battleground. The attempts by other tech giants to break Google's monopoly on the search cloud is another already much older battleground, but also a case for how difficult it is to bring down established empires. To this day, others do not seem to be able really to tear down the walls around the Google search empire, although Microsoft has gained ground and is now the second biggest search business in the USA.

But the fiercest battles, according to the *Economist* (2012), are about who will provide digital content to consumers. Digital music is currently Apple's domain, while e-books belong to Amazon. Still, both markets are heavily contested. Digital content is at the centre of most of the current battles and has become the main motivation of customers to purchase other products as well, which goes so far that 'content sold the hardware' (Economist, 2012). Facebook's strategy is here particularly interesting and by now copied by others. It offers its own ecosystem of social links with their large network value to others, so that these can sell more digital content. Its already cited collaboration with Netflix to push up sales of digital films among online friends is just one example. All the other web giants try to replicate this success by providing deep links between their various technologies. Google, for instance, uses its knowledge from its Google+ networks to improve its own search results and sell more digital content.

This battle over the consumption of digital content is also fought on the companies' mobile and cloud platforms. 'Platforms are the weapons with which the warring factions seek to rule their own lands and conquer new ones. Patents are the weapons with which they try straightforwardly to hurt their rivals' (Economist, 2012). The *Financial Times* explains the patent wars (Waters et al., 2012) as a land grab on new technologies and their commercial potentials, and sees an intellectual property rights arms race developing based on a war chest of patents. Microsoft has traditionally a strong position in patents, as has Apple, because it takes a while before a company can build up a significant portfolio of patents. Facebook and Google have responded by purchasing other companies' patents. The patent war fought in courts of many countries has truly become global, and more and more people demand a reform of the patent system altogether, which they see as outdated in the digital age.

On the surface, many of the current battles between major Internet companies are the legal battles the patent wars have become famous for. They are fought in courts with highly paid lawyers on all sides. We have seen, however, that behind the patent wars lie the other battlegrounds for domineering digital content and its crowds and clouds that generate network value. Andrejevic also identifies the crowds that drive these clouds. He argues that behind the battles on intellectual property rights, there are often much deeper divisions about the control of a whole environment such as YouTube (Andrejevic, 2009) and the free labour incorporated in it. As Andrejevic observes, it is often not the multimedia asset itself that motivates the lawsuits, but the surrounding information such as user data, connections to other sites, etc. This is important information in the world of social marketing, and digital asset holders would like to have it back from intermediaries such as YouTube or, in fact, Google as a whole.

For Andrejevic, the integration of YouTube has closed a circle around the network value that Google aims for. Andrejevic elaborates that when Google bought YouTube in 2006, it did not add to the company's vast earnings. It was less an economic decision and more one to close the circle in the digital ecosystem of Google by linking videos to relevant advertisers and content marketers such as Amazon or iTunes. Its networked infrastructure has moved on from portals and single sites to whole ecosystems. These connect free labour of many communities via cloud-based platforms and allow digital media and its user-added information to move freely between devices. With the digital media, the results of the 'monitoring and experimentation' (Andrejevic, 2009: 419) of the user behaviour on digital assets can be moved easily, and their context of use can be better understood. We have identified these as the productive basis of capital in the digital ecosystems, in order to foster a customer's 'behavior in computer agents; their tastes, preferences, patterns of consumption and response to advertising' (Waters et al., 2012: 420). Once these can be computationally reasoned with, they can help improve all parts of the digital ecosystem and help enclose it further, as the human agents in it are represented as perfect computational models.

Users add their culture to the digital media assets and companies try to make money from the tastes and preferences of users by enclosing them in their ecosystems. This is what the network value is about. Facebook, as seen, even sells culture to other companies.

> More generally, information, knowledge, and culture are being subjected to a second enclosure movement... The freedom of action for individuals who wish to produce information, knowledge, and culture is being systematically curtailed in order to secure the economic returns demanded by the manufacturers of the industrial information economy.
>
> (Benkler, 2006: 23)

Benkler assumes that this battle is mainly fought between those who own the content and those who distribute it. For him, high-technology firms are worried about the rules promoted by Hollywood to protect its film outputs from digital piracy. Since Benkler's book, we have seen the emergence of completely new ways of distributing digital content in ecosystems. The same high-technology firms that are in charge of the various logical layers of the web use these to seek 'enclosure'. Openness can go together with closed environments, as the digital ecosystems of Apple and others show on a daily basis. Apple and other hi-tech companies deliver a complex mixture of open and closed components on the web's logical layer, as analysed in Chapter 4. So, while we have seen, in the last ten years, attempts to break open the web's physical layers by de-monopolising broadband networks and by opening them to competition, the logical layers are seeing an ever-increasing push towards closures.

This chapter has concluded our discussion of digital ecosystems and the role of crowds and clouds in them by looking at the global workflows around digital content. Here, we first concentrated on the division of work between humans (crowds) and machines (clouds) in ecosystems. We needed to understand that we cannot rely on traditional analysis and critique of this division of work in political economy, as computers are different kinds of machines. We then continued with a discussion of the growing importance of data assets in these global workflows and how these involve free labour to enable network value to emerge. Data and content seek network value and therefore importance in the global networks. They aim at becoming the items that not only make a difference, but also that nobody else can do without any more. Google, for instance, has – at the moment at least – achieved this with its digital map assets, which have in turn galvanised other companies to achieve the same with their digital assets.

7

Conclusion

Writing this book has turned out to be a greater challenge than originally anticipated, as two concepts needed to be brought together that have proven to be at best vague in their definitions. In order to start explaining the emerging digital asset ecosystem, one cannot rely on fixed definitions of digital assets (media or other content) and/or digital ecosystems, and then in good academic tradition work oneself backwards to sort, explain and cluster phenomena based on these definitions. Both concepts – digital ecosystems and digital assets – have proven to be evasive and underspecified.

Right at the beginning, we saw how much of the current uncertainties about what constitutes a digital asset are linked to recent developments towards digital ecosystems. On the most general level, a digital asset is a digital object with value. In the past, this was too often identified with enriched digital files that have usable metadata and the appropriate rights attached to them. Such a definition works if one considers the digital asset management use case that is most commonly discussed in introductory books, i.e. bringing order to the heap of digital files in a larger organisation in government, business and elsewhere. But it seems to us that this use case, while still valid, will only be part of the story of digital media and asset management in the future, since digital ecosystems are emerging. Digital objects of any kind are taking centre stage in this change. Digital assets need to be understood as part of global networked workflows, where their production and consumption is closely integrated.

With the emerging digital ecosystems, digital asset management theory and practice needs to expand its attentions towards the driving forces behind this change. We have identified these as crowds and clouds, which determine the global workflows in the digital economy. These two names stem from the recent excitement of crowdsourcing and cloud computing, but they go so much further, according to our analysis. They indicate a much deeper change in the situation of the global digital network than just in these two specific application areas. There is, first of all, the development of the World Wide Web, as the most important digital network of our times, into more than just the means to exchange documents and into an application framework to exchange services, data and other things that will be added in the future. The second major development is the integration of human collective intelligence into this network. This is not just crowdsourcing or Web 2.0 but is much better described by Amazon's view on its own new infrastructure services, where the crowds are hidden and are just another service among the many other computing services Amazon has to offer.

As we have discussed again and again in this book, crowds go where clouds currently cannot go, but both work on the same problems and challenges. They work together on processing and analysing the data and content on the web that has become too big or too smart to be investigated by crowds or clouds alone. Big data has had many names in the past, from data deluge to data tsunami, but the name 'big data' seems to have stuck once it had left the narrower field of research computing and moved on to be a definite building block of the future digital economy and society.

Big data cannot be comprehended simply in terms of size. It needs to be understood in terms of the challenges it poses towards current computing infrastructures and the need to break these open. Big data asks for the crowds and clouds to be developed into the joint infrastructure that companies like Amazon envision. For digital asset management, this is reason enough to stay close to the discussions on big data. Maybe more importantly, big data would often be better termed 'big content' or even 'big media'. Even if the kind of big tabular and numerical data of financial institutions is not part of digital asset management, big media definitely is. Big media often hides in the most unexpected places, if, for instance, clinical data is big in terms of terabytes and petabytes, because 95 per cent of it is video-based.

Once big data had entered our discussions, we could go on to define the idea of digital ecosystems, as they are discussed as one of the answers of how crowds and clouds can be reconfigured to address the needs of big data. Digital ecosystems turned out to be one of those things that are easier done than said. The idea is now commonly used in the self-descriptions of the CEOs of digital media companies, of consultants in the digital economy and, last but not least, in the research that describes these developments. In all these, vague definitions of digital ecosystems dominate, but maybe it is exactly the vagueness of these definitions that helps bind together seemingly unrelated domains in the global digital economy and society. It definitely helped us understand the connections between them. As presented, digital ecosystems are used to describe technology company clusters such as the one developing around TechCity in London, or to present approaches to biologically inspired computing, or to analyse business links, etc.

To us, digital ecosystems were interesting as templates that help explain how crowds and clouds work together to form companies such as Facebook. In biological systems, digital ecosystems split up into communities, which live in habitats in order to form niches to survive in this world. Facebook's idea is similar, as it imagines user and developer crowds working together in their Facebook platform habitats to deploy and use services that define them. Chapter 2 finished with two practical examples of existing digital ecosystems in publishing and media. Both integrate producers and consumers of digital objects in workflows where the distinction between amateurs and experts disappear. Digital asset and media management systems are key to this transformation, because they are often the places where this integration and collaboration happens, and is stored and managed.

In Chapter 3, we investigated the technologies and digital methodologies that needed to have happened in order to enable the emergence of digital ecosystems and crowds and clouds. The first evolution was to make the Internet a good place for humans and machines alike. In particular, the machines had to do some catching up to feel at home on the web. This might surprise those, who might assume that it is the machines that rule the web, but it was originally designed to exchange documents for human consumption. What we have only recently seen is a web beyond that, a web of data or a semantic web where machines can also derive meaning from the underlying documents.

Chapter 3 focused especially on those technologies and methodologies that turned out to be effective means of the kind of web transformation we have just described. So, web services only started to work once they did not imply new protocols and infrastructures, but reused only the existing ones of the web and became ReSTful. APIs make these services accessible and weave the machine web together. We found that services and APIs made the web a better habitat to live in, and not just for machines. Humans also found it easier to work online as various technologies annihilated the different experience of desktop and web environment by making the web fully interactive, which had, as demonstrated, a particularly strong impact on the consumption of digital media on the web.

Once the foundations for the best possible web for machine and humans are laid, crowds and clouds can develop freely. Both offer collaboration opportunities, and Chapter 3 discussed not only the different levels on which these are presented, but also how crowds and clouds can be used to undermine the collaboration opportunities an open web would offer. The chapter finished with a brief look into what the future bears and how the infrastructure around clouds and crowds moves towards a web of things that also integrates the real world of things into the digital world. The full potential of an open ecosystem will be realised. But then, it also needs open content to flow freely between systems and other participants of the digital ecosystem.

Since the earliest days of the web, open content has been its advantage for some, and, for others, its curse. This conflict has only accelerated, since the web can be used to distribute open digital assets rather than point to real-world objects. Chapter 4 took this as a starting point and introduced the discussion and background of open content, using two rather radical definitions in order to understand what is entailed here. According to these, content is open if it can be freely (re)used. This idea of (re)use has become especially pertinent in two areas, where the taxpayer offers the money to produce open data: open government and open sciences. Both have emerged as the foremost playground for open data and content services and applications.

Use value (for others) is accepted in open science and government as the most important characteristic of open data and open content. There are, however, problems in defining the right use. Gurstein has introduced the idea of effective use to limit potentially negative impact from open data if only the most powerful and richest also have the right means to make use of it. Effective use demands not just distribution of the data, but also the means to exploit it and to set up an equality architecture or an architecture of participation, as O'Reilly has called it. Going back to the original Web 2.0 text of O'Reilly, we found that his model of an architecture of participation is, for him, the first Napster environment. Here, people share their resources to store and access content, but they do so largely without noticing and while continuing with their other work. The architecture of participation is not just one where everyone participates as peers and is intrinsic, but also one which disappears behind other everyday activities. The Napster ecosystem is fully open.

Apple is, for O'Reilly, on the wrong end of an architecture of participation, which might surprise some, considering that this company invented the systems of apps, whereby all can develop applications. Apple's ecosystem is about enclosure of content to keep it within the realm of its own crowds and clouds. Its own digital asset management system iTunes has very much enabled this, and we discussed in detail, for various digital media types, how the success of Apple in the digital media market relies on a range of options to open or close its ecosystem, depending on the particular digital media type that is used and traded. It is too simple to see in Apple just the opposite end of an equality architecture. One needs to look deep into the ways it deals with various types of content to understand its strategy as one of opening and closing content at the same time.

However, open content does not just have a problem with its opposite closed content. It also has a problem with itself if it simply becomes too much to handle. Faced with the deluge of open content, we have become used to letting others master our digital content. These others can be human, but are most likely of some kind of algorithmic provenance. Filtering programs and recommenders have become the main guardians to help us assess and evaluate the online content offerings. A 'filter bubble' might emerge that locks us into the way these algorithms want us to see the world. Open data becomes enclosed again, this time by the guardian algorithms. Chapter 4 concluded that these kinds of problems with open data can only be avoided if the data is embedded in an open environment. We presented one idea to create this, with global open linked data taking hold also in the digital asset management world.

Open data eventually leads to big data. We have met the big data debate throughout this book, but concentrated on it in Chapter 5. In order to understand big data, we first had to establish the difference between data, information and knowledge. Not all digital content is data; it might have to be transformed first into the basic facts that make a difference, which are what we see data as. In this process, crowds and clouds play a key role, especially when we are considering complex multimedia content assets. Not just in Chapter 5, but also in other parts of the book we identified the technologies to do that, from crowdsourcing to computational information extraction. These technologies support transforming the content into the three Vs that are needed to call something big data: volume, velocity and variety.

The history of big data teaches us that sharing models of data were replaced by collecting models, as the former did not seem commercially viable. NoSQL technologies have been developed to support collecting on the large scale. They allow the content to be taken as it is and just collect it. The other defining technology of big data is MapReduce, invented by Google, but taken up by many others. MapReduce has been developed for the kind of analytical model that big data wrangling requires. First, slice it into the relevant data you need, then roll the dice to run your analytics.

MapReduce is a generalisation of many big data activities, as we have seen. These activities have recently moved away from the original innovator in big data, which was big science and into business. Here, it is especially the burgeoning social media industries that push the big data agenda. They promise to their marketing customers that they can analyse the sentiments of social media users in order to find out whether these might like the latest difference in the brand. Sentiment analysis has delivered some promising results for marketing, but we have seen that there are still significant challenges to be overcome.

Other, maybe more surprising big data organisations are emerging fast. The USA retailer Walmart, for instance, has for quite a while been using data collected from its stores to improve its sales. Then there are governments. Their archives contain lots and lots of information, and their digitisation progresses fast. Governments, furthermore, have the advantage that they can enlist their populations to deliver them data in census records, health records and so on. They are privileged collectors of big data, but need to ensure that they are not identified by their citizens as Big Brother types that want to use the collected data mainly for control. The Snowden revelations in 2013 have simply brought into the limelight what has been going on for a while.

Many of the criticisms of big data address these Big Brother concerns and demonstrate what can be done if relatively innocent small data sets are combined in order to form part of larger control society efforts. The fiercest criticisms of big data, however, were (at least for now) addressed by those ideologues that see the end of all kinds of traditional theories if big data analytics starts with patterns, rather than concepts. This is a false claim and big data rather seems to challenge some established theories and lead to new theoretical insights, which only confirms the theories' continued relevance. Big data does not mean the end of theories, but the advent of new ones that help evolve the digital ecosystems of crowds and clouds.

The final chapter returned to the question of the emerging global workflows in the digital economy between humans and computers, a topic that is surprisingly underrepresented in discussions. The exceptions here are MIT economists, who relate the latest developments to the original questions of the division of work between humans and machines, which is something famous classical economists like Adam Smith and Karl Marx already considered to be key to the understanding of economies. We found that it is old questions that still occupy us today. For instance, the alienation of the worker from their work products still seems to be an unresolved challenge in the digital economy. It is, however, also clear that the old answers seem not to work either, as computers are different kind of machines. They are universal machines that allow creativity to be embedded directly in the workflows. Computers therefore should not be confused with those old Fordist assembly lines machines that stand for all the harm alienation did in the past.

In the global computing workflows, data is the new 'Intel Inside' and helps achieve a new kind of intelligence that even ten years ago seemed unthinkable. Cars can all of a sudden drive by themselves – not because they are able to reproduce drivers' intelligence, but because they now have access to vast amounts of data that help them assess a situation quickly. They are helped here by information from social media sites, voluntarily contributed by human labour, which takes pictures of junctions, analyses traffic flow, etc. We discussed in the final chapter how believers in a classical economy could not have understood how voluntary free labour could have contributed value to anything. Marx would definitely not have understood how value could have been created without exploitation, and for Smith, value was always linked to pain.

Furthermore, we have seen that also in the world of free digital labour, exploitation has always been at hand. From the modern Turkers and little pay for complicated tasks to early examples of exploitations in global massive online player games, free labour has never been just free and voluntary. Even open source is not simply the playground of computer nerds it might have been once, and has become integrated as a business strategy of many software companies who all hope that their digital assets will be the next big things that nobody can dispense of in the global digital ecosystem.

We have finally discovered the network value as an addition to the three types of value a digital asset might have from its beginnings. Next to the cultural, the social and the monetary value, it is the network value that seems to determine a digital asset's position in the global digital ecosystem. It measures how influential it is in the global network, how much it influences others and how much the global network cannot do without it any more. All the digital asset producers are racing to develop those assets that mirror the importance of Google Maps on the web, the Microsoft Office platform or the dominance of the iPad in the world of tablet computer. Once a company has reached this network dominance and defines the 20 per cent that has 80 per cent of influence, it will do all it takes in the 'games of thrones' to defend it.

Those who operate in digital ecosystems know this and have been involved for quite a while in fighting to achieve the 20 per cent and for as long as possible. A generation that grew up with challenging the dominance of Microsoft products in the desktop computer space is now turning this experience into the online space and using digital ecosystems as a way of promoting their own dominance. The most visible part has been, over the past few years, many high-profile patent battles. But the court is here an extension of the online struggles to gain as many assets as possible to cover all parts of the online space. Google did not buy YouTube for immediate financial reasons in 2006; it saw its service and in particular its strong links to active online crowds as a key component to grow Google's own ecosystem.

Most of the analysts of the 'game of thrones' between and within digital ecosystems agree that it is mainly about digital content assets (deAgonia et al., 2013). These assets include gaming assets, formerly analogue material such as books and newspapers, videos and other advanced multimedia assets. In general, Facebook, Amazon, Google, Microsoft and Apple are the most commonly cited names involved in these struggles. However, not just they but also many other smaller and less well-known companies are involved, not to mention governments, as the Snowden case has made clear. None of these has gained supremacy in any of the involved content areas yet, but we need to wait a few more years to be able to cast judgement here.

These final discussions of this book on the 'game of thrones' demonstrated that the debate on digital ecosystems will not go away any time soon. The metaphor of digital ecosystems has developed into a viable technical and business model, with concrete examples that demonstrate its workings. Mark Zuckerberg sees Facebook's success as intrinsically linked to its ecosystem, and Apple makes every attempt to close its environment so that its users, as far as possible, are locked in, thereby confirming the existence of a distinct Apple ecosystem. Microsoft, Google and Amazon have also created their distinct flavours of digital ecosystems.

Maybe digital ecosystems will not survive as a term, as another metaphor will prove stronger. However, the phenomenon that digital ecosystems describe will not go away, as crowds and clouds are together extending their global reach as an infrastructure to address the next generation data and digital economy needs. New types of clouds keep being developed. We have only seen the beginning of the push of web and data platforms and corresponding business models. The evolution of crowds into a platform is an even more recent appearance. As crowds offer options where clouds cannot offer any at the moment, and clouds seamlessly integrate crowds into the platforms, we are witnessing the emergence of new models for our digital living-together.

This book began as an investigation into a specific discipline and area: digital asset and media management. While it kept its focus on digital content, it then presented how digital assets of all kinds can also be seen as first examples for a much bigger change in the underlying infrastructure, which is made up of crowds and clouds. At the same time, digital content and media are at the heart of this change, as parts of ever more useful and economically desirable applications. Content, from traditional document assets to multimedia and game assets, has really become king in the digital ecosystem world. It is distributed much faster and more widely, and has, at the same time, new ideas of value attached to it. For digital asset and media management, we therefore live in exciting times, but only if this change is also better understood by its professionals, researchers and practitioners. They need to recognise that the use cases of digital asset and media management have gone beyond the walls of an organisation. Understanding digital assets and digital media has become about so much more than decoding the heap of digital objects any organisation amasses. It means following them through their web life cycle and the global workflows organised around them.

The traditional elements of digital asset and media management, which are metadata and information systems analysis, are as important as ever. They mainly deal with questions of interoperability and other technical aspects, and have been joined by new interests in digital curation and preservation or social information surrounding digital media as part of the core skills that digital asset and media managers need to have. Our understanding of the global workflows and infrastructures digital media is now part of is, however, still only at the beginning. This book has tried to contribute to this debate. Much more work needs to be done and new methods need to be specified. For instance, we need to understand better how we could use our traditional knowledge of how to follow and analyse data in an organisation to analyse data in the global workflows. Or we need to integrate user analysis in our understanding of the connections that web APIs provide. We have only started with this work, but the benefits are already apparent. We need to foster the exchange with related disciplines and interests, and keep working on the central position that content has in our digital lives.

References

Aitamurto, Tanja and Lewis, Seth C. (2013). Open innovation in digital journalism: examining the impact of Open APIs at four news organizations. *New Media & Society*, 15(2), 314–31.

Alag, Satnam and MacManus, Richard (2009). *Collective Intelligence in Action*: New York: Manning.

Allemang, Dean and Hendler, James (2011). *Semantic Web for the Working Ontologist: Effective Modeling in RDFS and OWL*. San Francisco, CA: Morgan Kaufmann.

Amatriain, Xavier (2012). More data or better models. *TechnoCalifornia*. Retrieved 10 October 2013, from *http://technocalifornia.blogspot.co.uk/2012/07/more-data-or-better-models.html*

Andersen, Per (2007). *What is Web 2.0?: Ideas, Technologies and Implications for Education* (Vol. 1). Bristol: JISC.

Anderson, Chris (2008a). The end of theory. *Wired Magazine*, 16.

Anderson, Chris (2008b). *Long Tail, the Revised and Updated Edition: Why the Future of Business is Selling Less of More*. New York: Hyperion.

Anderson, David P. (2004). *Boinc: A System for Public-resource Computing and Storage*. Proceedings. Fifth IEEE/ACM International Workshop on Grid Computing.

Anderson, David P, Cobb, Jeff, Korpela, Eric, Lebofsky, Matt and Werthimer, Dan (2002). SETI@home: an experiment in public-resource computing. *Communications of the ACM*, 45(11), 56–61.

Andrejevic, Mark (2009). 'Exploiting YouTube: contradictions of user-generated labor', in P. Snickars and P. Vonderau (eds), *The YouTube Reader* (Vol. 413). Stockholm.

Angles, Renzo and Gutierrez, Claudio (2008). Survey of graph database models. *ACM Computing Surveys (CSUR)*, 40(1), 1.

Armbrust, Michael, Fox, Armando, Griffith, Rean, Joseph, Anthony D, Katz, Randy et al. (2010). A view of cloud computing. *Communications of the ACM*, 53(4), 50–8.

Arthur, Magan (2005). Intro to Digital Asset Management: Just what is a DAM? Retrieved 10 October 2013, from *www.realstorygroup.com/Feature/124-DAM-vs.-DM*

Ashley, Kevin (2013). Thoughts before 'The Future of the Past of the Web'. Retrieved 12 December 2013, from *http://digitalcuration.blogspot.co.uk/2011/10/thoughts-before-future-of-past-of-web.html*

Auer, Sören, Bizer, Christian, Kobilarov, Georgi, Lehmann, Jens, Cyganiak, Richard and Ives, Zachary (2007). Dbpedia: a nucleus for a web of open data. *The Semantic Web* (pp. 722–35). Heidelberg: Springer.

Austerberry, David (2012). *Digital Asset Management.* Oxford: Focal Press.

Baek, Kanghui, Holton, Avery, Harp, Dustin and Yaschur, Carolyn (2011). The links that bind: uncovering novel motivations for linking on Facebook. *Computers in Human Behavior*, 27(6), 2243–8.

Baeza-Yates, Ricardo and Ribeiro-Neto, Berthier (1999). *Modern Information Retrieval* (Vol. 463). New York: ACM Press.

Barnett, Emma (2012). Google: Sergey Brin says his Facebook and Apple criticisms were 'distorted'. *The Daily Telegraph*. Retrieved 12 December 2013, from *www.telegraph.co.uk/technology/google/9211539/Google-Sergey-Brin-says-his-Facebook-and-Apple-criticisms-were-distorted.html*

BBC (2012). Inside Facebook. Retrieved 12 December 2013, from *www.dailymotion.com/video/xmso1d_mark-zuckerberg-inside-facebook-full-doc_tech*

BBC (2013). Reddit apologises for online Boston witch hunt. Retrieved 12 December 2013, from *www.bbc.co.uk/news/technology-22263020*

BCS (2006). Isn't it semantic? Interview with Tim Berners-Lee. Retrieved 12 December 2013, from *www.bcs.org/content/conWebDoc/3337*

Behrendt, Wernher (2012). The Interactive Knowledge Stack (IKS): a vision for the future of CMS. *Semantic Technologies in Content Management Systems* (pp. 75–90). Heidelberg: Springer.

Bell, Robert M. and Koren, Yehuda (2007). Lessons from the Netflix prize challenge. *ACM SIGKDD Explorations Newsletter*, 9(2), 75–9.

Benjamin, Solomon, Bhuvaneswari, R. and Rajan, P. (2007). Bhoomi: E–governance, or, an anti–politics machine necessary to globalize Bangalore? Retrieved 12 December 2013, from *http://casumm.files.wordpress.com/2008/09/bhoomi-e-governance.pdf*

Benkler, Yochai (2006). *The Wealth of Networks: How Social Production Transforms Markets and Freedom*. Yale, CT: Yale University Press.

Benkler, Yochai and Nissenbaum, Helen (2006). Commons-based peer production and virtue. *Journal of Political Philosophy*, 14(4), 394–419.

Bergman, Michael K. (2005). Untapped assets: the $3 trillion value of US enterprise documents. Retrieved 12 December 2013, from *http://mkbergman.com/wp-content/themes/ai3/files/DocValue/DocumentsValue050712.pdf*

Berners-Lee, Tim (2006). Linked data. Retrieved 12 December 2013, from *www.w3.org/DesignIssues/LinkedData.html*

Berners-Lee, Tim (2007). Giant global graph. Retrieved 7 November 2013, from *http://dig.csail.mit.edu/breadcrumbs/node/215*

Berners-Lee, Tim (2010). Long live the web. *Scientific American*, 303(6), 80–5.

Berners-Lee, Tim, Hendler, James and Lassila, Ora (2001). The semantic web. *Scientific American*, 284(5), 28–37.

Beyer, Mark A. and Laney, Douglas (2012). *The Importance of «Big Data»: A Definition*. Stamford, CT: Gartner.

BI Insider (2012). HTML5 vs. apps: why the debate matters, and who will win. Retrieved 28 December 2012, from *www.businessinsider.com/html5-vs-apps-why-the-debate-matters-and-who-will-win-2012-11*

Biehn, Neil (2013). The missing V's in big data: viability and value. *Wired*. Retrieved 12 December 2013, from *www.wired.com/insights/2013/05/the-missing-vs-in-big-data-viability-and-value*

bigdata-startups.com (2013). Big data best practice: Walmart is making big data part of its DNA. Retrieved 12 November 2013, from *www.bigdata-startups.com/BigData-startup/walmart-making-big-data-part-dna*

Bizer, Christian, Heath, Tom and Berners-Lee, Tim (2009). Linked data – the story so far. *International Journal on Semantic Web and Information Systems (IJSWIS)*, 5(3), 1–22.

Blank, Seth (2011). API Integration Pain Survey results. Retrieved 22 December 2011, from *www.yourtrove.com/blog/2011/08/11/api-integration-pain-survey-results*

Blanke, Tobias, Hedges, Mark and Dunn, Stuart (2009). Arts and humanities e-science – current practices and future challenges. *Future Generation Computer Systems*, 25(4), 474–80.

Blanke, Tobias and Kristel, Conny (2013). Integrating Holocaust Research. *International Journal of Arts and Humanities Computing*, 7(1–2), 41–57.

Bollier, David and Firestone, Charles M. (2010). *The Promise and Peril of Big Data*. Washington, DC: Aspen Institute, Communications and Society Program.

Borgman, Christine L. (2012). The conundrum of sharing research data. *Journal of the American Society for Information Science and Technology*, 63(6), 1059–78.

Borgman, Christine L., Wallis, Jillian C. and Mayernik, Matthew S. (2012). Who's got the data? Interdependencies in science and technology collaborations. *Journal of Computer Supported Cooperative Work*, 21(6), 485–523.

Bowker, Geoffrey C. (2005). *Memory Practices in the Sciences*. Cambridge, MA: MIT Press.

Bowman, Shayne and Willis, Chris (2003). We media: how audiences are shaping the future of news and information. Retrieved 12 December 2013, from *www.hypergene.net/wemedia/download/we_media.pdf*

Boyd, Danah and Crawford, Kate (2012). Critical questions for big data: provocations for a cultural, technological, and scholarly phenomenon. *Information, Communication & Society*, 15(5), 662–79.

Brin, Sergey (2012). Reply to 'Web freedom faces greatest threat ever, warns Google's Sergey Brin'. Retrieved 12 December 2013, from *https://plus.google.com/109813896768294978296/posts/44gsPvAm5a5*

Briscoe, Gerard and Sadedin, Suzanne (2009). Digital business ecosystems: natural science paradigms. *arXiv preprint arXiv:0910.0646*.

Briscoe, G., Sadedin, S. and De Wilde, W. (2011). Digital ecosystems: ecosystem-oriented architectures. *Natural Computing*, 10(3), 1143–94.

Brown, Eileen (2012). *Working the Crowd: Social Media Marketing for Business*. London: BCS, The Chartered Institute.

Brynjolfsson, Erik, Hu, Yu Jeffrey and Smith, Michael D. (2006). From niches to riches: the anatomy of the long tail. *Sloan Management Review*, 47(4), 67–71.

Brynjolfsson, Erik, Hu, Yu Jeffrey and Smith, Michael D. (2010). Research commentary – long tails vs. superstars: the effect of information technology on product variety and sales concentration patterns. *Information Systems Research*, 21(4), 736–47.

Brynjolfsson, Erik and McAfee, Andrew (2011). *Race Against the Machine: How the Digital Revolution is Accelerating Innovation, Driving Productivity, and Irreversibly Transforming Employment and the Economy*. Lexington, MA: Digital Frontier Press.

Brynjolfsson, Erik, McAfee, Andrew, Sorell, Michael and Zhu, Feng (2008). Scale without mass: business process replication and industry dynamics. *Harvard Business School Technology & Operations Management Unit Research Paper* (07–016).

Buyya, Rajkumar, Yeo, Chee Shin, Venugopal, Srikumar, Broberg, James and Brandic, Ivona (2009). Cloud computing and emerging IT platforms: vision, hype, and reality for delivering computing as the 5th utility. *Future Generation Computer Systems*, 25(6), 599–616.

California Health Interview Survey (2010). CHIS Making an Impact. Retrieved 11 November 2012, from *http://healthpolicy.ucla.edu/about/expert/Pages/chis_making_impact.pdf*

Callebaut, Werner (2012). Scientific perspectivism: a philosopher of science's response to the challenge of big data biology. *Studies in History and Philosophy of Science Part C: Studies in History and Philosophy of Biological and Biomedical Sciences*, 43(1), 69–80.

Carreiro, Erin (2010). Electronic books: how digital devices and supplementary new technologies are changing the face of the publishing industry. *Publishing Research Quarterly*, 26(4), 219–35.

Cellan-Jones, Rory (2013). Fail fast, move on – making government digital. BBC. Retrieved 12 December 2013, from *www.bbc.co.uk/news/technology-23354062*

Chang, Elizabeth and West, Martin (2006). *Digital Ecosystems: A Next Generation of the Collaborative Environment.* Paper presented at the Eight International Conference on Information Integration and Web-Based Applications & Services.

Chang, Fay, Dean, Jeffrey, Ghemawat, Sanjay, Hsieh, Wilson C., Wallach, Deborah A. et al. (2008). Bigtable: a distributed storage system for structured data. *ACM Transactions on Computer Systems (TOCS)*, 26(2), 4.

Choi, Hyunyoung and Varian, Hal (2012). Predicting the present with google trends. *Economic Record*, 88(s1), 2–9.

Clark, Jessica and Aufderheide, Patricia (2009). Public media 2.0: dynamic, engaged publics. Retrieved 12 December 2013, from *http://cmsimpact.org/sites/default/files/documents/pages/publicmedia2.0.pdf*

Columbus, Louis (2013). Gartner predicts infrastructure services will accelerate cloud computing growth. Forbes. Retrieved 12 December 2013, from *www.forbes.com/sites/louiscolumbus/2013/02/19/gartner-predicts-infrastructure-services-will-accelerate-cloud-computing-growth*

Cook, Samantha, Conrad, Corrie, Fowlkes, Ashley L. and Mohebbi, Matthew H. (2011). Assessing Google flu trends performance in the United States during the 2009 influenza virus A (H1N1) pandemic. *PLoS One*, 6(8), e23610.

Craig, Terence and Ludloff, Mary E. (2011). *Privacy and Big Data.* Sebastopol, CA: O'Reilly Media, Inc.

Crawford, Alejandro and Chau, Lisa (2013). Why Google's business model works. US News. Retrieved 12 December 2013, from *www.usnews.com/opinion/blogs/economic-intelligence/2013/06/25/why-googles-business-model-works*

Darrow, Barb (2012a). The Amazon API battle for the cloud rages on. Gigaom. Retrieved 12 December 2013, from *http://gigaom.com/2012/06/20/the-amazon-api-battle-for-the-cloud-rages-on*

Darrow, Barb (2012b). OpenNebula quietly keeps building its open-source cloud. Gigaom. Retrieved 12 December 2013, from *http://gigaom.com/2012/07/10/opennebula-quietly-keeps-building-its-open-source-cloud*

Daston, Lorraine (1991). The ideal and reality of the republic of letters in the Enlightenment. *Science in Context*, 4(2), 367–86.

Davies, Tim (2010a). Comment to 'Open Data: Empowering the Empowered or Effective Data Use for Everyone?'. Retrieved 12 December 2013, from *http://gurstein.wordpress.com/2010/09/02/open-data-empowering-the-empowered-or-effective-data-use-for-everyone/#comments*

Davies, Tim (2010b). *Open Data, Democracy and Public sector Reform.* Oxford: University of Oxford. Retrieved 12 December 2013, from *http://practicalparticipation.co.uk/odi/report/wp-content/uploads/2010/08/How-is-open-governmentdata-being-used-in-practice.pdf*

Davis, Kenan, Popovich, Nadja, Powell, Kenton, MacAskill, Ewen, Spencer, Ruth, & Gelder, Lisa van (2013). NSA Files: Decoded, *The Guardian.* Retrieved 12 December 2013, from *www.theguardian.com/world/interactive/2013/nov/01/snowden-nsa-files-surveillance-revelations-decoded*

deAgonia, Michael, Gralla, Preston and Raphael, J.R. (2013). Battle of the media ecosystems: Amazon, Apple, Google and Microsoft. Computerworld. Retrieved 12 December 2013, from *www.computerworld.com/s/article/9240650/Battle_of_the_media_ecosystems_Amazon_Apple_Google_and_Microsoft*

Dean, Jeffrey and Ghemawat, Sanjay (2008). MapReduce: simplified data processing on large clusters. *Communications of the ACM*, 51(1), 107–13.

DeCandia, Giuseppe, Hastorun, Deniz, Jampani, Madan, Kakulapati, Gunavardhan, Lakshman, Avinash et al. (2007). *Dynamo: Amazon's*

Highly Available Key-value Store. Paper presented at the ACM Symposium on Operating Systems Principles.

Deelman, Ewa, Gannon, Dennis, Shields, Matthew and Taylor, Ian (2009). Workflows and e-science: an overview of workflow system features and capabilities. *Future Generation Computer Systems*, 25(5), 528–40.

Deuze, Mark (2008). The changing context of news work: liquid journalism and monitorial citizenship. *International Journal of Communication*, 5(2), 848–65.

Deuze, Mark (2009). Media industries, work and life. *European Journal of Communication*, 24(4), 467–80.

Dibbell, Julian (2007). The life of the Chinese gold farmer. *The New York Times*. Retrieved 12 December 2013, from *www.nytimes.com/2007/06/17/magazine/17lootfarmers-t.html*

Dignan, Larry (2012). Amazon CEO Bezos: AWS is lean manufacturing, Kindle Fire for IT. ZDnet. Retrieved 12 December 2013, from *www.zdnet.com/amazon-ceo-bezos-aws-is-lean-manufacturing-kindle-fire-for-it-7000008115*

Dini, Paolo, Iqani, Mehita and Mansell, Robin (2011). The (im) possibility of interdisciplinarity: lessons from constructing a theoretical framework for digital ecosystems. *Culture, Theory and Critique*, 52(1), 3–27.

Dini, Paolo and Nicolai, A. (2007). A scientific foundation for digital ecosystems. Retrieved 12 December 2012, from *www.digital-ecosystems.org/book/papers/t1.0.pdf*

Doan, Anhai, Ramakrishnan, Raghu and Halevy, Alon Y. (2011). Crowdsourcing systems on the world-wide web. *Communications of the ACM*, 54(4), 86–96.

Dobo, Jozef and Steed, Anthony (2012). *3D Revision Control Framework*. Paper presented at the Proceedings of the 17th International Conference on 3D Web Technology, Los Angeles, CA.

Domingos, Pedro and Richardson, Matt (2001). *Mining the Network Value of Customers*. Paper presented at the Proceedings of the Seventh ACM SIGKDD International Conference on Knowledge Discovery and Data Mining, San Francisco, CA.

Dretske, Fred (1981). *Knowledge and the Flow of Information*. Cambridge, MA: MIT Press.

Dugas, Andrea Freyer, Hsieh, Yu-Hsiang, Levin, Scott R., Pines, Jesse M., Mareiniss, Darren P. et al. (2012). Google flu trends: correlation with emergency department influenza rates and crowding metrics. *Clinical Infectious Diseases*, 54(4), 463–9.

Dupre, John and Gagnier, Regenia (1996). A brief history of work. *Journal of Economic Issues*, 30(2), 553–9.

Eaton, Ben, Elaluf-Calderwood, Silvia, Sørensen, Carsten and Yoo, Youngjin (2011). *Dynamic Structures of Control and Generativity in Digital Ecosystem Service Innovation: The Cases of the Apple and Google Mobile App Stores*. London: London School of Economics and Political Science.

Economist (2010). Data, data everywhere. *The Economist*. Retrieved 12 December 2013, from *www.economist.com/node/15557443*

Economist (2011). The dangers of the Internet – invisible sieve. *The Economist*. Retrieved 12 December 2013, from *www.economist.com/node/18894910*

Economist (2012). Technology giants at war – another game of thrones. *The Economist*. Retrieved 12 December 2013, from *www.economist.com/news/21567361-google-apple-facebook-and-amazon-are-each-others-throats-all-sorts-ways-another-game*

Edwards, Paul N. (2003). 'Infrastructure and modernity: force, time, and social organization in the history of sociotechnical systems', in T.J. Misa, P. Brey and A. Feenberg (eds), *Modernity and Technology* (pp. 185–225), Cambridge, MA: MIT Press.

Eifrem, Emil (2009). Neo4j – the benefits of graph databases. *no: sql (east)*. Retrieved 12 October 2013, from *www.slideshare.net/emileifrem/nosql-east-a-nosql-overview-and-the-benefits-of-graph-databases*

Elkstein, Michael (2008). Learn REST: a tutorial. Retrieved 12 November 2010, from *http://rest.elkstein.org/2008/02/what-is-rest.html*

Feijóo, Claudio, Maghiros, Ioannis, Abadie, Fabienne and Gómez-Barroso, José-Luis (2009). Exploring a heterogeneous and fragmented digital ecosystem: mobile content. *Telematics and Informatics*, 26(3), 282–92.

Financial Times (2012a). Big data bonanza – the information revolution and the invisible hand. *The Financial Times*. Retrieved 12 December 2013, from *www.ft.com/cms/s/2/ed724876-45f8-11e2-b7ba-00144feabdc0.html-axzz2PzsJe14d*

Financial Times (2012b). How design persuades us to give up big data. *The Financial Times*. Retrieved 12 December 2013, from *http://video.ft.com/v/2033679761001/How-design-persuades-us-to-give-up-big-data-/Companies*

Finch Group Report (2012). Accessibility, sustainability, excellence: how to expand access to research publications. *Report of the Working Group on Expanding Access to Published Research Findings*. Retrieved

12 December 2013, from *www.researchinfonet.org/wp-content/uploads/2012/06/Finch-Group-report-FINAL-VERSION.pdf*

Fish, Adam (2011). *Governance of Labor in Digital Video Networks.* Paper presented at the Proceedings of the 2011 iConference.

Flasko, Elisa (2010). Windows Azure Marketplace – introducing DataMarket. Retrieved 11 January 2013, from *http://msdn.microsoft.com/en-us/magazine/gg309173.aspx*

Floridi, Luciano (2002). *Philosophy and Computing: An Introduction.* London: Routledge.

Fort, Karen (2011). Amazon Mechanical Turk: gold mine or coal mine? Retrieved 11 November 2013, from *http://crowdresearch.org/blog/?p=2135*

Foster, Ian, Zhao, Yong, Raicu, Ioan and Lu, Shiyong (2008). *Cloud Computing and Grid Computing 360-degree Compared.* Paper presented at the Grid Computing Environments Workshop, 2008. GCE'08.

Franklin, Michael J., Kossmann, Donald, Kraska, Tim, Ramesh, Sukriti and Xin, Reynold (2011). *CrowdDB: Answering Queries with Crowdsourcing.* Paper presented at the Proceedings of the 2011 ACM SIGMOD International Conference on Management of Data.

Garfinkel, Simson (2011). The cloud imperative. Retrieved 1 February 2013, from *www.technologyreview.com/news/425623/the-cloud-imperative*

Garrett, Jesse James (2005). Ajax: a new approach to web applications. Retrieved 12 December 2012, from *www.adaptivepath.com/ideas/ajax-new-approach-web-applications*

Gartner, Richard, L'Hours, Hervé and Young, Grant (2008). Metadata for digital libraries: state of the art and future directions. Retrieved 12 December 2013, from *www.jisc.ac.uk/media/documents/techwatch/tsw_0801pdf.pdf*

Garzarelli, Giampaolo, Limam, Yasmina Reem and Thomassen, Bjørn (2008). Open source software and economic growth: a classical division of labor perspective. *Information Technology for Development*, 14(2), 116–35.

Giles, Jim (2012). Twitter shows language evolves in cities. *The New Scientist.* Retrieved 12 December 2013, from *www.newscientist.com/article/mg21628916.300-twitter-shows-language-evolves-in-cities.html*

Gill, Timothy (2005). USA Patent No. 6947959. United States Patent.

Gillmor, Dan (2008). *We the Media: Grassroots Journalism by the People, for the People.* Sebastopol, CA: O'Reilly Media, Inc.

Gitelman, Lisa (2013). *Raw Data Is an Oxymoron*. Cambridge, MA: MIT Press.

Glaser, Hugh and Millard, Ian (2009). Linked Data: Publishing and Consuming on the Semantic Web. Seminar at Tsinghua-Southampton Web Science Laboratory at Shenzhen, Shenzhen, PRC. Retrieved 12 December 2013, from *http://eprints.soton.ac.uk/267788/1/Shenzhen-2009-08-19.pdf*

Gottlieb, Seth (2008). Content is not data. Retrieved 12 December 2013, from *http://contenthere.net/2008/05/content-is-not-data.html*

Gowers, Timothy (2012). Elsevier – my part in its downfall. Retrieved 1 October 2013, from *http://gowers.wordpress.com/2012/01/21/elsevier-my-part-in-its-downfall*

Grimes, Seth (2011). Unstructured data and the 80 percent rule. Retrieved 2 January 2013, from *www.clarabridge.com/default.aspx?tabid=137&ModuleID=635&ArticleID=551*

Grinter, Beki (2013). A big data confession. *Interactions*, 20(4), 10–11. doi: 10.1145/2486227.2486231.

Gurstein, Michael (2003). Effective use: a community informatics strategy beyond the digital divide. *First Monday*, 8(12), 1–18.

Gurstein, Michael (2007). *What is Community Informatics (and Why Does it Matter)?* (Vol. 2), Milan: Polimetrica.

Gurstein, Michael (2011). Open data: empowering the empowered or effective data use for everyone? *First Monday*, 16(2).

Habermas, Jürgen, Lennox, Sara and Lennox, Frank (1974). The public sphere: an encyclopedia article (1964). *New German Critique* (3), 49–55.

Halevy, Alon, Norvig, Peter and Pereira, Fernando (2009). The unreasonable effectiveness of data. *IEEE Intelligent Systems*, 24(2), 8–12.

Halliday, Josh (2012). Facebook stops New Year message tool. *The Guardian*. Retrieved 12 December 2013, from *www.guardian.co.uk/technology/2012/dec/31/facebook-disables-new-year-message-app*

Hand, Eric (2011). Culturomics: word play. *Nature*, 474(7352), 436–40.

Hanna, Richard, Rohm, Andrew and Crittenden, Victoria L. (2011). We're all connected: the power of the social media ecosystem. *Business Horizons*, 54(3), 265–73.

Harris, Robin (2013). Can big data make government cheaper?, ZDnet. Retrieved 12 December 2013, from *www.zdnet.com/can-big-data-make-government-cheaper-7000018191*

Harrison, C., Eckman, B., Hamilton, R., Hartswick, P., Kalagnanam, J., Paraszczak, J. and Williams, P. (2010). Foundations for smarter cities. *IBM Journal of Research and Development*, 54(4), 1–16.

Heath, Tom and Bizer, Christian (2011). Linked data: evolving the web into a global data space. *Synthesis Lectures on the Semantic Web: Theory and Technology*, 1(1), 1–136.

Hey, Anthony J.G., Tansley, Stewart and Tolle, Kristin Michele (2009). Redmond, WA: Microsoft Research.

Hinchcliffe, Dion (2008). Comparing Amazon's and Google's Platform-as-a-Service (PaaS) offerings. ZDnet. Retrieved 12 December 2013, from *www.zdnet.com/blog/hinchcliffe/comparing-amazons-and-googles-platform-as-a-service-paas-offerings/166*

HM Government (2012). Working definition of public data. Retrieved 2 March 2013, from *http://data.gov.uk/opendataconsultation/annex-2*

Hof, Robert D. (2006). Jeff Bezos' Risky Bet. *Bloomberg Business Magazine*. Retrieved 12 December 2013, from *www.businessweek.com/stories/2006-11-12/jeff-bezos-risky-bet*

Hoffmann, Alexander (2012). State of Apple's ecosystem lock-in. Retrieved 12 December 2013, from *www.macgasm.net/2012/02/09/state-apples-ecosystem-lockin*

Holley, Rose (2010). Crowdsourcing: how and why should libraries do it? *D-Lib Magazine*, 16(3/5). *www.dlib.org/dlib/march10/holley/03holley.html*

Homo Luddite (2011). Invisible autopropaganda. Retrieved 2 March 2013, from *http://homoluddite.wordpress.com/2011/07/06/in-praise-of-filter-bubbles*

Horton, John J. (2011). The condition of the Turking class: are online employers fair and honest? *Economics Letters*, 111(1), 10–12.

Howe, Jeff (2006). The rise of crowdsourcing. *Wired Magazine*, 14(6), 1–4.

IEEE Digital Ecosystem (2007). Digital ecosystem. Retrieved 2 January 2013, from *www.ieee-dest.curtin.edu.au/2007*

Ipeirotis, Panagiotis G. (2010). Analyzing the Amazon Mechanical Turk marketplace. *XRDS: Crossroads, The ACM Magazine for Students*, 17(2), 16–21.

Irani, Lilly C. and Silberman, M. Six (2013). *Turkopticon: Interrupting Worker Invisibility in Amazon Mechanical Turk*. Paper presented at the Proceedings of the SIGCHI Conference on Human Factors in Computing Systems, Paris, France.

Ivanov, Ivan I. (2009). Utility computing: reality and beyond. *E-business and Telecommunications* (pp. 16–29). Heidelberg: Springer.

Jacobs, Adam (2009). The pathologies of big data. *Communications of the ACM*, 52(8), 36–44.

Jacobsen, Jens, Schlenker, Tilman and Edwards, Lisa (2005). *Implementing a Digital Asset Management System: for Animation, Computer Games, and Web Development*. New York: Taylor & Francis US.

Jaeger, Paul T., Lin, Jimmy, Grimes, Justin M. and Simmons, Shannon N. (2009). Where is the cloud? Geography, economics, environment, and jurisdiction in cloud computing. *First Monday*, 14(5).

Janert, Philipp K. (2010). *Data Analysis with Open Source Tools*. Sebastopol, CA: O'Reilly Media, Inc.

Jansen, Bernard J, Zhang, Mimi, Sobel, Kate and Chowdury, Abdur (2009). Twitter power: tweets as electronic word of mouth. *Journal of the American Society for Information Science and Technology*, 60(11), 2169–88.

Jenkins, Jack (2012). Facebook midnight delivery security flaw. Retrieved 1 February 2013, from *http://jcj9.wordpress.com/2012/12/31/facebook-midnight-delivery-security-flaw*

Jordanous, Anna (2010). *Defining Creativity: Finding Keywords for Creativity Using Corpus Linguistics Techniques*. Paper presented at the Proceedings of the First International Conference on Computational Creativity.

Jung, Gwangjae and Lee, Byungtae (2010). *Analysis on Social Network Adoption According to the Change of Network Topology: The Impact of Open API to Adoption of Facebook*. Paper presented at the Proceedings of the 12th International Conference on Electronic Commerce: Roadmap for the Future of Electronic Business.

Jung, Keechul, Kim, Kwang In, and Jain, Anil K. (2004). Text information extraction in images and video: a survey. *Pattern Recognition*, 37(5), 977–97.

Kahn, Gilles, Bertot, Yves, Huet, Gérard and Lévy, Jean-Jacques (2009). *From Semantics to Computer Science: Essays in Honour of Gilles Kahn*. Cambridge: Cambridge University Press.

Kalakota, Ravi (2012). Amazon Web Services. Retrieved 3 March 2013, from *http://cloudblueprint.wordpress.com/2012/04/26/amazon-web-services-aws*

Katz, Ian (2012). Web freedom faces greatest threat ever, warns Google's Sergey Brin. *The Guardian*. Retrieved 12 December 2013, from *www.guardian.co.uk/technology/2012/apr/15/web-freedom-threat-google-brin*

Kauppi, Niilo (2003). Bourdieu's political sociology and the politics of European integration. *Theory and Society*, 32(5–6), 775–89.

Kelly, Jeff (2012). Google playing the big data long game. Retrieved 12 December 2013, from *http://wikibon.org/blog/google-playing-the-big-data-long-game*

Kittur, Aniket and Kraut, Robert E. (2008). *Harnessing the Wisdom of Crowds in Wikipedia: Quality Through Coordination.* Paper presented at the Proceedings of the 2008 ACM Conference on Computer Supported Cooperative Work.

Kobilarov, Georgi, Scott, Tom, Raimond, Yves, Oliver, Silver, Sizemore, Chris et al. (2009). Media meets semantic web – how the BBC uses dbpedia and linked data to make connections. *The Semantic Web: Research and Applications* (pp. 723–37). Heidelberg: Springer.

Kon, Martin, Gosalia, Sujata and Portelette, Edouard (2010). A new digital future for publishers? Retrieved 12 December 2013, from *www.oliverwyman.com/media/OW_EN_CMT_PUBL_2010_NewDigitalFuture.pdf*

Kurz, Thomas, Schaffert, Sebastian, Guentner, Georg and Fernandez, Manuel (2012). *Adding Wings to Red Bull Media: Search and Display Semantically Enhanced Video Fragments.* Paper presented at the Proceedings of the 21st International Conference Companion on World Wide Web, Lyon, France.

Latour, Bruno (1990). Drawing things together. *The Map Reader: Theories of Mapping Practice and Cartographic Representation*, 65–72.

Latour, Bruno (2005). From realpolitik to dingpolitik. Introduction to *Making Things Public: Atmospheres of Democracy*. Cambridge, MA: MIT Press.

Le Bon, Gustave (1897). *The Crowd: A Study of the Popular Mind.* New York: Macmillan.

LeFurgy, Bill (2012). Life cycle models for digital stewardship. Retrieved 10 October 2013, from *http://blogs.loc.gov/digitalpreservation/2012/02/life-cycle-models-for-digital-stewardship*

Lemley, Mark A. (2011). Is the sky falling on the content industries? *J. on Telecomm. & High Tech. L.*, 9, 125.

Lenk, Alexander, Klems, Markus, Nimis, Jens, Tai, Stefan and Sandholm, Thomas (2009). *What's Inside the Cloud? An Architectural Map of the Cloud Landscape.* Paper presented at the Proceedings of the 2009 ICSE Workshop on Software Engineering Challenges of Cloud Computing.

Lerman, Jonas (2013). Big data and its exclusions. *Stanford Law Review Online*, 66, 55.

Levy, Frank and Murnane, Richard J. (2012). *The New Division of Labor: How Computers are Creating the Next Job Market*. Princeton, NJ: Princeton University Press.

Lichtenberg, James (2010). Signal or noise: what can we learn from all these digital publishing conferences? *Publishing Research Quarterly*, 26(2), 110–3.

Lintott, Chris J., Schawinski, Kevin, Slosar, Anže, Land, Kate, Bamford, Steven et al. (2008). Galaxy Zoo: morphologies derived from visual inspection of galaxies from the Sloan Digital Sky Survey. *Monthly Notices of the Royal Astronomical Society*, 389(3), 1179–89.

Lohman, Tim (2013). Open Knowledge Foundation launches Australian chapter. ZDnet. Retrieved 12 December 2013, from *www.zdnet.com/open-knowledge-foundation-launches-australian-chapter-7000019928*

Lohr, Steve (2012). The age of big data. *The New York Times*, 11.

Lycett, Mark (2013). 'Datafication': making sense of (big) data in a complex world. *European Journal of Information Systems*, 22(4), 381–6.

Lyman, Peter and Varian, Hal R. (2003). How much information? Retrieved 2 January 2013, from *www.sims.berkeley.edu/how-much-info-2003*

Lynch, Clifford (2008). Big data: how do your data grow? *Nature*, 455(7209), 28–9.

MacManus, Richard (2007). Social graph and beyond: Tim Berners-Lee's graph is the next level. Retrieved 1 February 2013, from *http://readwrite.com/2007/11/22/social_graph_tim_berners-lee*

Malone, Thomas, Laubacher, Robert and Dellarocas, Chrysanthos (2009). Harnessing crowds: mapping the genome of collective intelligence. Retrieved 12 December 2013, from *http://cci.mit.edu/publications/CCIwp2009-01.pdf*

Manovich, Lev (2011). 'Trending: the promises and the challenges of big social data', in M.K. Gold (ed.), *Debates in the Digital Humanities* (pp. 460–75). Minneapolis, MN: University of Minnesota Press.

Mansell, Robin (2004). Political economy, power and new media. *New Media & Society*, 6(1), 74–83.

Manyika, James, Chui, Michael, Brown, Brad, Bughin, Jacques, Dobbs, Richard, Roxburgh, Charles and Byers, Angela Hung (2011). Big data: the next frontier for innovation, competition, and productivity. *McKinsey Global Institute*, 1–137, from *www.mckinsey.com/insights/business_technology/big_data_the_next_frontier_for_innovation*

Marshall, Cathy (2012). Big data, the crowd and me. *Information Services and Use*, 32(3), 215–26.

Marx, Karl (1867). *Capital, volume I.* Harmondsworth: Penguin/New Left Review.

Mayer-Schönberger, Viktor and Cukier, Kenneth (2013). *Big Data: A Revolution that Will Transform How We Live, Work, and Think.* Boston, MA: Houghton Mifflin Harcourt.

McIntyre, David P. and Subramaniam, Mohan (2009). Strategy in network industries: a review and research agenda. *Journal of Management*, 35(6), 1494–1517.

McKendrick, Joe (2008). How to tap into the largest SOA in the world. Retrieved 1 October 2013, from *www.zdnet.com/blog/service-oriented/how-to-tap-into-the-largest-soa-in-the-world/1072*

McMillan, Robert (2012). Amazon delivers coal to Netflix watchers on Christmas Eve. *Wired.* Retrieved 12 December 2013, from *www.wired.com/wiredenterprise/2012/12/amazon-outag*

McNally, Michael B. (2010). Enterprise content management systems and the application of Taylorism and Fordism to intellectual labour. *Ephemera: Theory & Politics in Organization*, 10(3/4), 357–73.

McNamee, Roger (2012). HTML 5: the next big thing for content. Retrieved 1 October 2013, from *http://rogerandmike.com/post/24006177542/html5-the-next-big-thing-for-content*

Mell, Peter and Grance, Timothy (2011). The NIST definition of cloud computing. *NIST* special publication, 800, 145.

Mohanty, Soumendra, Jagadeesh, Madhu and Srivatsa, Harsha (2013). 'Big data' in the enterprise. *Big Data Imperatives* (pp. 1–24). Heidelberg: Springer.

MyCustomer (2000). Marriage of giants as AOL and Amazon tie the knot. Retrieved 2 December 2012, from *www.mycustomer.com/topic/technology/marriage-giants-aol-and-amazon-tie-knot*

Nariani, Rajiv and Fernandez, Leila (2012). Open access publishing: what authors want. *College & Research Libraries*, 73(2), 182–95.

Naughton, John (2006). Blogging and the emerging media ecosystem. Background paper for an invited seminar to Reuters Fellowship. Retrieved 2 February 2012, from *http://reutersinstitute.politics.ox.ac.uk/fileadmin/documents/discussion/blogging.pdf*

Naughton, John (2013). To the internet giants, you're not a customer. You're just another user. *The Guardian.* Retrieved 12 December 2013, from *www.theguardian.com/technology/2013/jun/09/internet-giants-just-another-customer*

Netflix Tech Blog (2010). Four reasons we choose Amazon's cloud as our computing platform. Retrieved 12 December 2013, from *http://techblog.netflix.com/2010/12/four-reasons-we-choose-amazons-cloud-as.html*

Newfield, Christopher (2013). Corporate open source – intellectual property and the struggle over value. *Radical Philosophy*, 181, 6–11.

Nielsen, Nikolaj (2013). US cloud snoops pose questions for EU cybercrime body. *EUObserver*. Retrieved 12 December 2013, from *http://euobserver.com/justice/118677*

Nietzsche, Friedrich Wilhelm (2005). *Thus Spoke Zarathustra: A Book for Everyone and Nobody*. Oxford: Oxford University Press.

O'Reilly, Tim (2004). The architecture of participation. Retrieved 12 December 2012, from *www.oreillynet.com/pub/a/oreilly/tim/articles/architecture_of_participation.html*

O'Reilly, Tim (2005). What Is Web 2.0 – design patterns and business models for the next generation of software. Retrieved 12 December 2012, from *http://oreilly.com/web2/archive/what-is-web-20.html*

O'Reilly, Tim (2007). What is Web 2.0: design patterns and business models for the next generation of software (updated version). *Communications & Strategies* (1), 17.

Okolloh, Ory (2009). Ushahidi, or 'testimony': Web 2.0 tools for crowdsourcing crisis information. *Participatory Learning and Action*, 59(1), 65–70.

Oomen, Johan and Aroyo, Lora (2011). *Crowdsourcing in the Cultural Heritage Domain: Opportunities and Challenges*. Paper presented at the Proceedings of the 5th International Conference on Communities and Technologies.

Open Knowledge Foundation (2011). Open definition. Retrieved 12 December 2012, from *http://opendefinition.org/okd*

Pang, Bo and Lee, Lillian (2008). Opinion mining and sentiment analysis. *Foundations and Trends in Information Retrieval*, 2(1–2), 1–135.

Pariser, Eli (2011). *The Filter Bubble: What the Internet is Hiding from You*. New York: Penguin.

Pasquinelli, Matteo (2009). Google's PageRank algorithm: a diagram of cognitive capitalism and the rentier of the common intellect. *Deep Search*, 152–62.

Pavolotsky, John (2012). Demystifying big data. *Business Law Today*, Retrieved 12 December 2012, from *www.jurimetrics.org/buslaw/blt/content/2012/11/article-03-pavolotsky.pdf*

Pearson, Helen (2001). Biology's name game. *Nature*, 411(6838), 631–2.

Perez, Juan (2007). Google wants your phonemes. Retrieved 1 October 2012, from *www.infoworld.com/t/data-management/google-wants-your-phonemes-539*

Pilászy, István and Tikk, Domonkos (2009). *Recommending New Movies: Even a Few Ratings are More Valuable than Metadata.* Paper presented at the Proceedings of the Third ACM conference on Recommender Systems, New York, USA.

Pollock, Rufus (2013). Forget big data – small data is the real revolution. Retrieved 12 December 2012, from *http://blog.okfn.org/2013/04/22/forget-big-data-small-data-is-the-real-revolution*

Poole, Steven (2013). Facebook Home wants your data, but don't worry: just lie to it now and then. *The Guardian.* Retrieved 12 December 2012, from *www.guardian.co.uk/commentisfree/2013/apr/05/facebook-home-wants-your-data*

Pouilloux, François (2011). *Extracting Named Entities at Web Scale for Competitive Intelligence.* Paper presented at the IEEE/WIC/ACM International Conference on Web Intelligence and Intelligent Agent Technology (WI-IAT).

Preston, Peter (2012). Newsweek's gone online, and Rupert's iPad Daily's just gone. *The Guardian.* Retrieved 12 December 2012, from *www.guardian.co.uk/media/2012/dec/09/newsweek-goes-online-the-daily-closes-murdoch*

Procter, Rob, Crump, Jeremy, Karstedt, Susanne, Voss, Alex and Cantijoch, Marta (2013a). Reading the riots: what were the police doing on Twitter? *Policing and Society: An International Journal of Research and Policy*, 23(4), 1–24.

Procter, Rob, Vis, Farida and Voss, Alex (2013b). Reading the riots on Twitter: methodological innovation for the analysis of big data. *International Journal of Social Research Methodology*, 16(3), 197–214.

Ramana, U.V. and Prabhakar, T.V. (2005). *Some Experiments with the Performance of LAMP Architecture.* Paper presented at the Fifth International Conference on Computer and Information Technology (CIT).

Redman, Thomas C. (2008). *Data Driven: Profiting from Your Most Important Business Asset.* Boston, MA: Harvard Business Press.

Redmond, E., Wilson, J.R. and Carter, J. (2012). *Guide to Modern Databases and the NoSQL Movement.* Raleigh, NC: Pragmatic Programmers, LLC.

Redmond, Eric, Wilson, Jim R. and Carter, Jacquelyn (2012). *Seven Databases in Seven Weeks: A Guide to Modern Databases and the NoSQL Movement.* Dallas, TX: Pragmatic Bookshelf.

Reeves, Joshua Howard (2013). *If You See Something, Say Something: Surveillance, Communication, and Citizenship in American Life.*

Raleigh, NC: North Carolina State University. Retrieved 12 December 2013, from *http://repository.lib.ncsu.edu/ir/bitstream/1840.16/8762/1/etd.pdf*

Regalado, Antonio (2013). Just don't call it big data. *The Technology Review*. Retrieved 12 December 2013, from *www.technologyreview.com/view/515941/just-dont-call-it-big-data*

Resnick, Paul and Varian, Hal R. (1997). Recommender systems. *Communications of the ACM*, 40(3), 56–8.

Rhodes, Matt (2010). The problem with automated sentiment analysis. Retrieved 12 December 2013, from *www.freshnetworks.com/blog/2010/05/the-problem-with-automated-sentiment-analysis*

Robles, Patricio (2012). Five legitimate use cases for NoSQL databases. Retrieved 1 October 2013, from *http://econsultancy.com/uk/blog/10654-five-legitimate-use-cases-for-nosql-databases*

Rogers, Simon (2010). Information is power. *The Guardian*. Retrieved 12 December 2013, from *www.theguardian.com/media/2010/may/24/data-journalism*

Rohrer, Finlo (2013). Vine: six things people have learned about six-second video in a week. *The BBC News Magazine*. Retrieved 12 December 2013, from *www.bbc.co.uk/news/magazine-21267741*

Ross, Joel, Irani, Lilly, Silberman, M. Zaldivar, Andrew and Tomlinson, Bill (2010). *Who are the Crowdworkers?: Shifting Demographics in Mechanical Turk*. Paper presented at the Proceedings of the 28th of the International Conference on Human Factors in Computing Systems, Extended Abstracts.

Rouvroy, Antoinette and Poullet, Yves (2009). The right to informational self-determination and the value of self-development: reassessing the importance of privacy for democracy. *Reinventing Data Protection?* (pp. 45–76). Heidelberg: Springer.

Rowley, Jennifer (2005). Building brand webs: customer relationship management through the Tesco Clubcard loyalty scheme. *International Journal of Retail & Distribution Management*, 33(3), 194–206.

Sadalage, Pramod J. and Fowler, Martin (2012). *NoSQL Distilled: A Brief Guide to the Emerging World of Polyglot Persistence*. Boston, MA: Addison-Wesley Professional.

Saleh, Tamim, Brock, Jon, Yousif, Nadjia and Luers, Andrew (2013). The age of digital ecosystems: thriving in a world of big data. Retrieved 12 December 2013, from *www.bcgperspectives.com/content/articles/information_technology_strategy_digital_economy_age_digital_ecosystems_thriving_world_big_data*

Schadt, Eric E. (2012). The changing privacy landscape in the era of big data. *Molecular Systems Biology*, 8(1).

Schaffert, Sebastian, Bauer, Christoph, Kurz, Thomas, Dorschel, Fabian, Glachs, Dietmar and Fernandez, Manuel (2012). *The Linked Media Framework: Integrating and Interlinking Enterprise Media Content and Data.* Paper presented at the Proceedings of the 8th International Conference on Semantic Systems.

Scheithauer, Gregor, Voigt, Konrad, Winkler, Matthias, Bicer, Veli and Strunk, Anja (2011). Integrated service engineering workbench: service engineering for digital ecosystems. *International Journal of Electronic Business*, 9(5), 392–413.

Schnapp, Jeffrey Thompson and Tiews, Matthew (2006). 'Introduction', in J.T. Schnapp and M. Tiews (eds), *Crowds* (pp. IX–XVI). Stanford, CA: Stanford University Press.

Scholz, Trebor (2012). *Digital Labor: The Internet as Playground and Factory.* New York: Routledge.

Schradie, Jen (2013). Big data not big enough? How the digital divide leaves people out. *MediaShift.* Retrieved 12 December 2013, from *www.pbs.org/mediashift/2013/07/big-data-not-big-enough-how-digital-divide-leaves-people-out*

Serbanati, Luca Dan, Ricci, Fabrizio L., Mercurio, Gregorio and Vasilateanu, Andrei (2011). Steps towards a digital health ecosystem. *Journal of Biomedical Informatics*, 44(4), 621–36.

Shadbolt, Nigel, O'Hara, Kieron, Berners-Lee, Tim, Gibbins, Nicholas, Glaser, Hugh and Hall, Wendy (2012). Linked open government data: lessons from Data.gov.uk. *IEEE Intelligent Systems*, 27(3), 16–24.

Sharma, Bhanu, Thulasiram, Ruppa K., Thulasiraman, Parimala, Garg, Saurabh K. and Buyya, Rajkumar (2012). *Pricing Cloud Compute Commodities: A Novel Financial Economic Model.* Paper presented at the Proceedings of the 2012 12th IEEE/ACM International Symposium on Cluster, Cloud and Grid Computing (ccgrid 2012).

Shirts, Michael and Pande, Vijay S. (2006). Screen savers of the world unite. *COMPUTING*, 10, 43.

Smith, Adam (1999). *The Wealth of Nations (Books I–III).* London: Penguin.

Smith, Matthew, Szongott, Christian, Henne, Benjamin and von Voigt, Gabriele (2012). *Big Data Privacy Issues in Public Social Media.* Paper presented at the Sixth IEEE International Conference on Digital Ecosystems Technologies (DEST).

Sorokin, Alexander and Forsyth, David (2008). *Utility Data Annotation with Amazon Mechanical Turk.* IEEE Computer Society Conference on Computer Vision and Pattern Recognition Workshops, 2008 (CVPRW'08).

Star, Susan Leigh (1992). The Trojan door: organizations, work, and the open black box. *Systems Practice*, 5(4), 395–410.

Stark, Nathan J. (1964). The public's concern for professional competence. *JAMA: The Journal of the American Medical Association*, 189(1), 27–30.

Stringfly (2013). Stringfly. Retrieved 1 October 2013, from *www.stringfly.com*

Suber, Peter (2010). Open access overview. Retrieved 12 December 2012, from *www.earlham.edu/~peters/fos/overview.htm*

Surowiecki, James (2005). *The Wisdom of Crowds*. New York: Anchor Books.

Sweney, Mark (2012). News Corp to close iPad newspaper *The Daily*. *The Guardian*. Retrieved 12 December 2012, from *www.guardian.co.uk/media/2012/dec/03/news-corp-close-ipad-the-daily*

Tönnies, Ferdinand (1955). *Community and Association (Gemeinschaft und gesellschaft)*. London: Routledge & Paul.

Tuomi, Ilkka (1999). *Data is More than Knowledge: Implications of the Reversed Knowledge Hierarchy for Knowledge Management and Organizational Memory*. Paper presented at the Thirty-second Annual Hawaii International Conference on System Sciences.

Ulieru, Mihaela and Verdon, John (2009). *Organizational Transformation in the Digital Economy*. Paper presented at 7th IEEE International Conference on Industrial Informatics (INDIN).

Van Dijck, José and Poell, Thomas (2013). Understanding social media logic. *Media and Communication*, 1(1), 2–14.

Von Ahn, Luis, Maurer, Benjamin, McMillen, Colin, Abraham, David and Blum, Manuel (2008). reCAPTCHA: human-based character recognition via web security measures. *Science*, 321(5895), 1465–8.

Walter, Mark (2004). Architectural considerations in digital asset management. *The Gilbane Report, Tech. Rep*, Retrieved 12 December 2012, from *http://gilbane.com/whitepapers.pl?view=12*

Wampler, Dean and Clark, Tony (2010). Guest editors' introduction: multiparadigm programming. *Software, IEEE*, 27(5), 20–4.

Wampler, Dean, Clark, Tony, Ford, Neal and Goetz, Brian (2010). Multiparadigm programming in industry: a discussion with Neal Ford and Brian Goetz. *Software, IEEE*, 27(5), 61–4.

Wang, Lizhe, Von Laszewski, Gregor, Younge, Andrew, He, Xi, Kunze, Marcel, Tao, Jie and Fu, Cheng (2010). Cloud computing: a perspective study. *New Generation Computing*, 28(2), 137–46.

Waters, Richard, Jones, Cleve and Sivathasan, Nalini (2012). What are the patent wars? *The Financial Times*. Retrieved 12 December 2013, from *www.ft.com/cms/s/0/165e9aee-3e35-11e2-91cb-00144feabdc0.html-axzz2FQTwuIrR*

Web 3.0 (2007). GGG, WWW, 123. Retrieved 10 October 2013, from *http://web3next.blogspot.co.uk/2007/11/ggg-www-123.html*

Webber, Jim, Parastatidis, Savas and Robinson, Ian (2010). *REST in Practice: Hypermedia and Systems Architecture*. Sebastopol, CA: O'Reilly Media, Inc.

Whitehorn, Mark (2013). Tell me, professor, what is big data? *The Register*. Retrieved 12 December 2013, from *www.theregister.co.uk/2013/08/12/big_data_for_big_problems_analysis*

Whittaker, Zack (2012). How much data is consumed every minute? Retrieved 1 February 2013, from *www.zdnet.com/blog/btl/how-much-data-is-consumed-every-minute/80666*

Widen (2012). Our digital asset management software as a service solution – the media collective. Retrieved 1 February 2013, from *www.widen.com/digital-asset-management-software-as-a-service*

Wiegand, Michael, Balahur, Alexandra, Roth, Benjamin, Klakow, Dietrich and Montoyo, Andrés (2010). *A Survey on the Role of Negation in Sentiment Analysis*. Paper presented at the Proceedings of the Workshop on Negation and Speculation in Natural Language Processing.

Wikipedia (2013a). Duck typing. Retrieved 12 December 2013, from *http://en.wikipedia.org/wiki/Duck_typing*

Wikipedia (2013b). Free software. Retrieved 12 December 2013, from *http://en.wikiquote.org/wiki/Free_software*

Wikipedia (2013c). NoSQL. Retrieved 12 December 2013, from *http://en.wikipedia.org/wiki/NoSQL*

Wikipedia (2013d). Open notebook science. Retrieved 12 December 2013, from *http://en.wikipedia.org/wiki/Open_notebook_science*

Williams, Christopher (2012). Netflix: the online cinema that wants to read your mind. *The Daily Telegraph*. Retrieved 12 December 2013, from *www.telegraph.co.uk/technology/news/9171714/Netflix-the-online-cinema-that-wants-to-read-your-mind.html*

Wilson, Thomas D. (2002). The nonsense of knowledge management. *Information Research*, 8(1), 1–8.

Wittaker, Zack (2012). Bruce Willis to take on Apple over iTunes inheritance. CBS News. Retrieved 12 December 2013, from *www.cbsnews.com/8301-501465_162-57505159-501465/bruce-willis-to-take-on-apple-over-itunes-inheritance*

World Economic Forum (2007). Digital ecosystem convergence. Retrieved 1 October 2013, from *www.weforum.org/reports/digital-ecosystem-convergence-between-it-telecoms-media-and-entertainment-scenarios-2015*

Yiotis, Kristin (2013). The open access initiative: a new paradigm for scholarly communications. *Information Technology and Libraries*, 24(4), 157–62.

Yu, Shuli and Woodard, C. Jason (2009). *Innovation in the Programmable Web: Characterizing the Mashup Ecosystem.* Paper presented at the Service-Oriented Computing–ICSOC 2008 Workshops.

Zhang, Guo and Jacob, Elin K. (2011). *Places for Digital Ecosystems, Digital Ecosystems in Places.* Paper presented at the Proceedings of the International Conference on Management of Emergent Digital EcoSystems.

Zins, Chaim (2007). Conceptual approaches for defining data, information, and knowledge. *Journal of the American Society for Information Science and Technology*, 58(4), 479–93.

Zittrain, Jonathan (2008). Ubiquitous human computing. *Philosophical Transactions of the Royal Society A: Mathematical, Physical and Engineering Sciences*, 366(1881), 3813–21.

Index

Kolibri 360 GmbH
Ferdinand-Jühlke-Straße 7
99095 Erfurt, Deutschland
produktsicherheit@kolibri360.de